D1268158

WHAT IS DOGMA?

CHARLES JOURNET

WHAT IS DOGMA?

Translated by
Mark Pontifex, O.S.B.

With an Introduction by
Roger W. Nutt

IGNATIUS PRESS   SAN FRANCISCO

Original French edition:
Le Dogme chemin de la Foi
©1963 by Librairie Artheme Fayard

Original English edition:
©1964 by Hawthorn Books, Inc., New York
Printed by permission of the Foundation du Cardinal Journet
Printed with ecclesiastical approval

Cover photo
Saint Peter's Square
© iStockphoto

Cover design by: Roxanne Mei Lum

© 2011 by Ignatius Press, San Francisco
All rights reserved
ISBN 978-1-58617-246-6
Library of Congress Control Number 2008936290
Printed in the United States of America ♾

CONTENTS

FOREWORD

The Life and Legacy of Charles Journet

The life of Charles Journet and his writings manifest a unified message—both convey a happy co-mingling of scholarly penetration and contemplative wisdom. Journet was born in Geneva, Switzerland in 1891 and was ordained to the priesthood in 1917. After an initial period of service as the pastor of a parish, Fr. Journet spent his entire fifty-six year academic career teaching dogmatic theology at the major seminary of the Diocese of Fribourg in Switzerland, while also sustaining a prolific career as a Catholic writer and spiritual guide. Even though Journet was intensely engaged in his writing and teaching career, he continued to exercise his priestly ministry and offer spiritual guidance on the weekends in Geneva. He also fostered deep spiritual friendships with many notable Catholics, including Jacques and Raïssa Maritain.

Journet wrote on a wide variety of theological topics including book-length treatments of the Church, evil, the Eucharist, grace, Mary, and this volume on dogma. Among these many publications, his multi-volume tome in ecclesiology, *L'Eglise du Verbe incarné* (*The Church of the Word Incarnate*), is considered his greatest single contribution; this work was described by noted twentieth-century theologian Yves Cardinal Congar, O.P., as the greatest ecclesiological work of the first half of the twentieth century.

Though Journet's writings cover many diverse topics, each flows fluidly from a common theological foundation by virtue of their author's acute awareness of the Trinitarian and Christological roots of the Christian faith, and the complimentary rapport that exists between the orders of faith and reason. Like the theology of his great inspiration, St. Thomas Aquinas, Journet's publications are not reaching attempts at novelty; indeed, his writings are ordered by the wisdom of God that is communicated in divine revelation and refracted through the theological patrimony of the Church. This sapiential spirit is precisely what endows Journet's work with its timeless value.

As the twentieth century moved along, Journet's theological work gained such recognition that Pope Paul VI elevated him to the Episcopacy and College of Cardinals in February of 1965. Cardinal Journet took an active role in the final session of the Second Vatican Council, making important contributions to the Council's treatment of religious freedom, and the indissoluble character of the Sacrament of Matrimony that is elaborated in the *Constitution on the Church in the Modern World* (*Gaudium et Spes*).

A full generation has now elapsed since Journet's death at the age of eighty-four in 1975, and uniquely as the time passes, appreciation and recognition of his work and legacy continues to increase. A number of his books, sometimes fifty years after their original appearance in French, have recently been translated into English for the first time or, like this book, are being printed again. Besides the patrimony of his own writings, Journet left something else as well, and its sustained existence is further evidence of the richness of his theological vision. In 1926 Journet co-founded the theological journal *Nova et Vetera*. The phrase *nova et vetera* (which means "new things and old things") was borrowed by Journet from Matthew 13:52, wherein Jesus says, "Therefore every scribe who has been trained for the kingdom of heaven is like a householder who brings out of his treasure what is new [*nova*] and what is old [*vetera*]." These words exhibit the theological spirit of the journal and its co-founder. Consistent with his lifelong pastoral sensitivity and academic concerns, Journet's purpose for *Nova et Vetera* was to cast the light and clarity of the Gospel upon contemporary problems and events.

Over seventy-five years since its inaugural volume, *Nova et Vetera* is still published and is highly respected. After Journet's death the reach of the journal has expanded well beyond the French speaking world. Alongside the French edition, *Nova et Vetera* has been published in Italian, and in 2002 the Aquinas Center for Theological Renewal at Ave Maria University, under the co-editorship of Dr. Matthew Levering and Dr. Michael Dauphinais, began publishing a very robust English edition.

The Enduring Value of What Is Dogma?

This small volume, *What is Dogma?*, is just as needed today—perhaps even more so—as it was nearly fifty years ago when Journet wrote it. The period after the Second Vatican Council has been a time when dogma, as well as many dogmas, have been "under fire" or denied outright by numerous Catholic theologians and faithful. Closely following the theology of St. Thomas Aquinas, Journet's understanding of the nature of faith enabled him to savor dogma as the mediated communication of the wisdom of God. Faith, which assents to the truths presented in revelation, is a "prophetic light" in which God "tells us" about himself and his plan for us through dogmas or foundational truths which seek "to stir up each human being to assent to his own redemption" (p. 23). Dogmas of faith are not adolescent formulations or human constructs imposed on us by those in power "they are", Journet explains, "paths which lead to God" (p. 31).

In this book, Journet explains the meaning of faith, which the Letter to the Hebrews defines as "the assurance of things hoped for" (Heb 11:1), as the unfolding of prophetic truths embodied in the dogmas proclaimed by the Church. He presents us with the unity of the truths of faith and those truths about God that the human mind has the natural ability to come to know (preambles). Following divine revelation, Journet identifies two truths—that God is and that he rewards those who seek him (see Heb 11:6)—as the foundational "credibilia" of faith. Journet provides helpful examples rooted in Sacred Scripture of dogmatic development as the faith organically unfolds from the foundational credibilia to profound dogmatic mysteries like the Triune God and the Real Presence of Christ in the Eucharist. This volume ends with a brief chapter—much too brief—on dogma and contemplation. Such an ending is an apt summary of Journet's approach to theology and life. A true understanding of Christian theology and dogma does not reduce the mysteries of faith to the realm of experience or banish them to the unknowable. Authentic Christian theology, embodied in the work of Charles Cardinal Journet, uses the mind's speculative powers, prophetically enlightened and sanctified by faith, to probe ever more deeply and prayerfully into the wisdom of God.

In the preface to the English edition of another of Journet's books,[1] Georges Cardinal Cottier, O.P., himself a great Swiss Thomist and Journet's hand-selected successor as the Director of *Nova et Vetera*, made the following observation: "May this little work increase in many the desire to study the theology of Charles Journet, a great theologian whose work has still not received the attention that it deserves." Those words equally apply to this volume. It is my hope that the republication of *What Is Dogma?* contributes to the ongoing dissemination of Charles Journet's insights, and through his insights, to a deeper prayerful appreciation of the life of faith and Christian dogma. As of this writing, the journal is published under the auspices of the Augustine Institute of Denver, Colorado.

Note on the current edition

With few exceptions, this volume simply reproduces the very fine translation of Mark Pontifex, O.S.B, published in 1964. A comparison with the French original revealed a small number of minor errors in the first English edition, which have been corrected in the current edition.

Roger W. Nutt
Ave Maria, Florida

---

[1] *The Theology of the Church*, trans. Victor Szczurek, O. Praem. (San Francisco: Ignatius Press, 2004), p. xxix.

INTRODUCTION

Who are you, Lord?
—Acts 9:5
For now we see in a mirror dimly,
but then face to face.
— 1 Cor 13:12

There are two aspects of faith; it has two kinds of light, which are inseparable and complementary: the prophetic light presents to us what we are to believe, and the sanctifying light, by making us assent to what we should believe, becomes "the foundation and source of all justification".[1] It is the former kind of light which concerns us here, not indeed exclusively, but principally. Certainly it is the less important kind, but yet it is absolutely necessary, and without it no act of faith would be possible, without it the virtue of faith would lie dormant in us, as in a baptized child.

I shall first try to trace it out even in its most hidden forms. I shall then describe briefly the way in which it developed in the Old Testament and in the apostolic period when it was expressed in new revelations. Then, in the

[1] Council of Trent, Session 6, chap. 8; Denzinger 801.

post-apostolic age, the canonical revelation, being completed, could only be made more explicit, and so the advance of revelation was followed by its fuller unfolding; articles of faith were followed by dogmas or truths of faith.

It will be necessary to pause at this point, to give some examples of dogmatic development, to show how, without being subjected to a particular culture, dogma can sometimes pass beyond commonsense views, while remaining in contact with their soundest elements. Next we shall have to emphasize the absolute truth of revealed truths, which is yet compatible with development in their formulation, then to notice, without giving names, one or two examples of those who have gone astray in modern times, and then to quote the words of Pope John XXIII describing the way in which doctrine can be taught and error suppressed in our own time.

Finally, we must try to come down to those great sections of the human race among which the fullness of the revealed message has become weakened, to say a few words about the sad case of the Catholic who gives up his belief, and lastly, to draw attention to the life and wonderful appreciation of dogma in the contemplative soul.

Fribourg, Whitsun 1963

CHAPTER I

Are Dogmas an Object of Faith?

The Object of Faith Is Both Wholly within Us and Wholly outside Us

Writers should cease to quote St. Thomas[1] against this, making him say that through faith we are aware of looking, not at the formula, but at the truth of the living God.[2] What would the truth of faith be, if it were not conformity of a statement with reality? There can be no mistake about the thought of St. Thomas, the very way in which he puts the question about the object of faith shows the meaning of his answer. It is twofold: the object of faith is outside us as referring to the simplicity of divine Truth; the object of faith is within us as referring to the complexity of a statement. The object of faith is both the statement so far as this touches reality and reality so far as this is shown in the statement. It is both the statement to which faith assents and reality that becomes open to it by its assent, toward which it tends, and in which it terminates.[3] "Some

---

[1] "The act of the believer does not terminate in the statement but in the real" (IIa–IIae, Q. 1, art. 2, ad 2). It is the word "terminate" that St. Thomas means to emphasize.

[2] Phrases of this kind are to be found frequently in contemporary Catholic writings.

[3] IIa–IIae, Q. 1, art. 2; and *De veritate*, Q. 14, art. 8, ad 5 and 12.

people have supposed that faith is not concerned with the statement but with reality, *non est de enuntiabili sed de re.* . . . This is false, for faith involves assent, and hence it involves a judgment based on the true and the false: *non potest esse nisi de compositione, in qua verum et falsum invenitur.*[4]

The way is at once closed to those who would boast of their faith in the transcendent subject, which, as they say, speaks to us by means of human words. They wish—and the illusion is not a new one—to think it possible, thanks to the progress of knowledge, to give the dogmas of the Church a meaning different from that which the Church has given them and gives them.[5]

Dogmas Are Essentially Unchangeable

It was in the attempt to solve a somewhat subtle difficulty that certain medieval thinkers were led to maintain that statements are not an object of faith. The ancient world, writes St. Augustine, looked forward to the Savior; we believe that he has come: "times have changed, not the faith"; *tempora variata sunt, non fides.*[6] Today it is no longer true to say that Christ will be born; time has made us alter the statement, which thus cannot share in the unchangeableness of faith. St. Thomas expresses this by saying that statements of faith exclude a changeableness that is essential, but not one that is accidental.[7] In the

---

[4] *De Veritate*, Q. 14, art. 12.
[5] First Vatican Council, Session 3, chap. 4, can. 3; Denz. 1818.
[6] *Enarr. in Ps* L, 17. cf. I *Sent.* dist. 41, expositio textus.
[7] III *Sent.*, dist. 24, art. 1, Q. 2, ad 5.

present instance the essential point is that there is a time for Christ's birth, and that this time does not change; the accidental point is that this time is future or past in relation to us.[8]

It is this essential identity of what faith believes, in spite of accidental modifications, that explains how the faith, still general and implicit in the ancients, is the same as the precise and explicit faith of the moderns: "without it the Church would no longer be one",[9] and equally explains how a council could restate a Symbol of faith, in order to explain it better.[10]

Knowledge and Love

There is this difference between faith and charity, that faith, being knowledge, reaches reality only by means of judgments to which it is required to give interior assent, while charity, being love, casts us upon reality just as it is outside of us, in pure simplicity.[11] And that is why, St. Thomas goes on to observe, in view of the present imperfection of our knowledge, it is better here below to love God rather than to know him; *melior est amor Dei quam cognitio.*[12]

[8] *De Veritate*, Q. 14, art. 12, ad 3.

[9] Ibid., art. 12.

[10] IIa–IIae, Q. 1, art. 10, ad 2.

[11] "The object of charity, the good, is in the real; the object of faith, the true, is gained by an activity of the soul. . . . That which is complex enters into the object of faith, that which is not complex is the object of charity." St. Thomas, III *Sent.*, dist. 24, Q. 1, art. 1, Q. 2, ad 3.

[12] I, Q. 83, art. 3.

Nevertheless love would be stifled without knowledge; knowledge opens the way for love. Charity has need of faith. It is true that on the path of faith it can go further than faith. It is natural to it to pass beyond faith. Here should be quoted the comparison with the ants. "The ant", says Ruysbroeck,

> does not make new paths, but all follow the same way, and, when the time comes, become capable of flight. . . . So too is it with those who live amid the stirrings of love. They will never make fresh paths or seek unusual ways of acting, but in spite of every tempest they will follow the way of love to the place to which love leads them. And then, in due time, by persevering in all the virtues, they will be able to see God and to be carried up within his mystery.[13]

When the love of the absolute, in order the better to attain its end, deliberately tries to set aside what faith reaches, when, thinking to go beyond this, it simply leaves it aside, it is certainly not the absolute of the God of revelation that it will meet at the end of its journey, but another absolute, another Spirit, which will frustrate its desires, in proposing to fulfill them.

---

[13] *The Adornment of the Spiritual Marriage.*

CHAPTER II

The Twofold Light of Faith

The Prophetic Light and the Sanctifying Light

If God loves us, if he wishes to make us love him, he must first reveal to us his mystery, and he must also give us the power to assent to it. Hence a twofold light is necessary: one that tells us what God is, his loving design for men, what he expects from them, by what paths they may come to him; another that permits them to raise up their minds so as to grasp "what no eye has seen, nor ear heard, nor the heart of man conceived, what God has prepared for those who love him" (1 Cor 2:9).

The first kind of light shows the lot of a humanity joined together in the same disaster, but saved by the same redemption. We may call this, in the broadest sense, a *prophetic* light. The second kind of light seeks in a hidden way to stir up each human being to assent to his own redemption. We may call this a *sanctifying* light. On the one hand, there is a prophetic light, which tells us what to believe, the statements of faith; on the other hand, there is a sanctifying light, that of theological faith and its act, which, by means of these statements, pierces and illuminates the night of God's mystery and of his providence.

This distinction between two kinds of light, one prophetic and the other sanctifying, is found even in the preaching of the Savior.

This Twofold Light Is Bestowed by Jesus

He is the subsisting Word, in which the Father, knowing himself, expresses himself and declares himself: "In the beginning was the Word, and the Word was with God, and the Word was God" (Jn 1:1), the Word, which is identified with essential love—"God is love" (1 Jn 4:8)—which cannot be uttered in God without producing the Holy Spirit. Love that is a person: the first love, by which the Father and the Son love one another, produces the second, rather as the tree produces its foliage,[1] the Word that is thus not only light, but light producing Love.[2]

The words of God are like his subsisting Word,[3] and that is why the Word made flesh, offering to men the prophetic light of his message, seeks, provided they place no obstacle in the way, to rouse in them the assent of faith, which will open to them the gates of another world: "If you continue in my word, you are truly my disciples, and you will know the truth, and the truth will make you free" (Jn 8:31).

The gospel is full of this twofold light: that of public preaching which can be refused, that of private assent which saves and sanctifies.

---

[1] "Sicut arbor florens floribus", St. Thomas, I, Q. 37, art. 2.

[2] "Verbum non qualecumque, sed spirans amorem" (ibid., Q. 43, art. 5, ad 2).

[3] "All the words of God are, as it were, a likeness of his Word", St. Thomas, *In symb. apost. expos.*, ed. Marietti, 895.

The word of God, received by one who does not grasp it, is the seed that fell on good ground (Mt 13:18–23). The threats of the owner of the vineyard stir the hate of the wicked vine-dressers (Mt 21:33–34). The invitation to the feast is scorned (Mt 22:1–14): "The light has come into the world, and men loved darkness rather than light, because their deeds were evil" (Jn 3:19). "'For this I have come into the world, to bear witness to the truth. Everyone who is of the truth hears my voice.' Pilate said to him, 'What is truth?'" (Jn 18:37–38).

Yet, while being declared outwardly, the word of God is also spoken in men's hearts. If Jesus rejected outwardly the prayer of the Canaanite woman, it was only to test her love: "O woman, great is your faith! Let it be done for your desire" (Mt 15:28). To the apostle's profession of faith he replies: "Blessed are you, Simon Bar-Jona! For flesh and blood has not revealed this to you, but my Father who is in heaven" (Mt 16:17). "Did not our hearts burn within us while he talked to us on the road, while he opened to us the Scriptures?" (Lk 24:32). "He came to his own home, and his own people received him not. But to all who received him, who believed in his name, he gave power to become children of God" (Jn 1:11–12). "Jesus said to the twelve, 'Will you also go away?' Simon Peter answered him, 'Lord, to whom shall we go? You have the words of eternal life" (Jn 6:67). "Jesus ... having found him he said, 'Do you believe in the Son of man?' He answered, 'And who he is, sir, that I may believe in him'" (Jn 9:35–36). "I know my own and my own know me" (Jn 10:14). "I do not pray for these only, but also for those who believe in me through their word"

(Jn 17:20). God has borne witness to his Son, and "he who believes in the Son of God has the testimony in himself" (1 Jn 5:10).

The prophetic light that tells us what we must believe, and the sanctifying light which saves us by making us believe it, enlightened the apostles.

The Prophetic Light and the Apostles

The prophetic light came directly upon the apostles as in earlier days upon the prophets. Abraham at the time of the covenant (Gen 17:1), Moses at Sinai (Ex. 19), Isaiah in the temple (Is 6:1), Ezekiel by the river Chebar (Ezek 1:1), John the Baptist at the baptism of Jesus (Jn 1:33), through the overwhelming power of a prophetic light received a message which they were to pass on to their own generations. In the overwhelming power of the prophetic light of Pentecost (Acts 2), of the appearance at Damascus (9:3), of the vision at Patmos (Rev. 1:10), the apostles, when the promise of the Old Testament was fulfilled in Jesus, understood the message that they were sent to teach all nations, even to the end of time (see Mt 28:18–20).

The light which enlightened them helped them in two ways, first to conceive in their own minds what God wished to make them know concerning his mystery and his design. That is the prophetic light of revelation. It also helped them to give outward expression to this revelation by speech or writing, and this is the prophetic light of inspiration through preaching or the Scriptures.

By the prophetic light of revelation (*apocalypsis*), God, "in him we live and move and have our being" (Acts 17:28), could, without using any violence, act upon the apostles' intellectual powers, whether in the order of objective presentation, or in that of subjective influence, so as to make them, through sensible emotions and images, form a judgment which was expressed on the intellectual level, and was communicable to other men, and in which God tells us about the mystery of his being and of his redemptive design.[4]

By the prophetic light of inspiration (*theopneustia*)[5] God could move the apostles, each in accordance with his character, so that each might communicate to others, without the least change, by speech or by writing, the mysteries of a salvation which concerns the whole human race. I say "by speech or by writing", though the usual reference is to the inspiration of Scripture,[6] because the apostle was equally assured of inspiration in his preaching and in his writing: "But even if we, or an angel from heaven, should preach to you a gospel contrary to that which we preached to you, let him be accursed" (Gal 1:8). And: "For I received from the Lord what I also delivered to you . . ." (1 Cor 11:23). And again: "Now I would remind you, brethren, in what terms I preached to you the gospel, which you received, in which you stand, by which you are saved, if you hold it fast—unless you believed in vain" (1 Cor 15:1–2).

---

[4] As to the way in which the Catholic idea of revelation differs both from the anthropomorphic idea and the modernist idea, see A. Gardeil, *Le donné révélé et la théologie* (Paris: Gabalda), pp. 41–76.

[5] Cf. 2 Tim 3:16.

[6] Leo XIII, Encyclical *Providentissimus*; Denz. 1952.

Is the Prophetic Light Communicable?

It was through an incommunicable prophetic experience that the apostles received a prophetic message which was communicable.

If by the word of God we mean the action by which God, through a twofold prophetic light, first causes the statements in which he tells us what he is and the designs of his providence, to be pronounced infallibly in the mind of the apostles (light of revelation), and afterwards to receive an infallible, external, formulation (light of inspiration) from them (though they might be given help by disciples such as Mark and Luke), then the word of God is an incommunicable experience.

If by the word of God we mean the statements in which an infallible result is caused by the prophetic light addressed to the apostles—or partially to their helpers—then the word of God is emphatically *communicable*.

The Sanctifying Light and the Apostles

The prophetic words in which God told the apostles what he is and the designs of his providence remain, *for them as for us, profoundly mysterious*, until there dawns the full brightness of the beatific vision: "Truly, you are a God who hide yourself, O God of Israel, the Savior" (Is 45:15). The apostles, like ourselves, were told to believe these mysteries in the darkness: "O the depth of the riches and wisdom and knowledge of God, how unsearchable are his judgments and how inscrutable his ways! 'For who has known the mind of the Lord, or who has been his counselor?'" (Rom 11:33–34). The unfathomable riches of Christ's wisdom which he is sent to announce to the gentiles, the plan of the mystery kept hidden in God from the beginning and which must now be set in the light, these are not seen, but believed, by the apostle, "in Christ Jesus our Lord, in whom we have boldness and confidence of access through our faith in him" (Eph 3:11–12). This is not yet the time for full knowledge: "For now we see in a mirror dimly, but then face to face. Now I know in part; then I shall understand fully, even as I have been fully understood. So faith, hope, love abide, these three; but the greatest of these is love" (1 Cor 13:12–13).

"Therefore, behold, I will allure her, and bring her into the wilderness, and speak tenderly to her" (Hos 2:14). This is true of every soul, and it is true of the apostles. If by the word of God we now mean the word which he pronounces in the apostles, giving them, through the sanctifying light of theological faith and the gifts of the Holy Spirit, power *to be the first to assent to the mysteries to which the statements revealed in them lead*, power to give inner acceptance, each in his measure, to the invitation addressed to them as to all men, then this sanctifying word of God remains the secret of each of them; it might well add some fervor to their preaching, but, like every word that is directly sanctifying, it remains essentially incommunicable. It is only in the next world that we shall see St. John's reply of personal faith to the unfathomable revelation of the Word made flesh, or the assent of St. Paul to Christ, who struck him down on the road to Damascus.

Can Man Now Speak the Word of God?

It is impossible for us to speak the prophetic word of God, in the same way that God spoke it in and through the apostles, but we can, and should at all times and places, speak this word and no other: "Go therefore and make disciples of all nations, ... teaching them to observe all that I have commanded you" (Mt 28:19).

The sanctifying word of God, by which he infuses into our hearts the assent of theological faith and of love, is, as I have just said, essentially personal and incommunicable. It was through supreme love that Jesus came to bring us the truth. The truth of God is always betrayed when it is offered without the love of God. The apostles preached, moved by a great love: "But we were gentle among you, like a nurse taking care of her children. So, being affectionately desirous of you, we were ready to share with you not only the gospel of God but also our own selves, because you had become very dear to us" (1 Thess 2:7–8). The faithful, when they heard them, must have felt their hearts burning within them, as at Emmaus; we are told that the Lord opened the heart of Lydia, the seller of purple goods, so that she should listen to Paul (Acts 16:14). Even then, even at the time of Jesus, the word of God found enemies. It is mysterious, hard to accept; it requires from us the death of many things that are very dear to us. As we well know, to preach it with but a faint love is to obscure it and to become responsible for many failures. Since our love will never rise to the level of Jesus' love, never even to the level of that of the apostles, in this sense it is true that we shall never be able to speak the word of God without some measure of betrayal.

Likeness between the Prophetic Light and the Sanctifying Light

1. Both lights, the prophetic and the sanctifying, are essential to faith. Both are supernatural, both come from above. But they are not of equal value; the sanctifying light is more precious. In the same way both body and soul are essential to man, but the soul is of greater value.

The prophetic light opens the paths which lead to God; the sanctifying light stirs us to pass over the threshold, and enables us to meet God.

The one is normally intended for all to know; the other is offered to each one in secret.

The one invites us to communion with God in Christ, the other is an answer to this invitation.

The first kind of light is offered from without, and awaits an answer, remaining still at a distance; the second kind of light, being theological, involves an inner assent to God, who reveals what he is and what are all things.

When the two lights appear at once in the same man, for example in St. John, who both reveals to the world the Word made flesh and also believes the Word made flesh, this man is greater through the light that makes him a believer, than through the light that makes him a prophet.

Now, as we know, the more precious light, that which forms believers, is offered directly and at once to all; while the light that forms prophets is only given directly to particular men, and only mediately to others.

2. These two kinds of light are temporary, both intended to strengthen, here below, the weakness of our eyes, which are unable to sustain God's brightness. The one brings to us the obscure statements in which is formulated God's mystery; the other raises our understanding to pierce the obscurity of the statements to which it assents. When the time of the final manifestation comes, the statements will vanish before the direct vision. At the same time the theological light of faith will be changed to a stronger light, allowing the soul to raise its eyes to God himself, the light of glory: "It does not yet appear what we shall be, but we know that when he appears we shall be like him, for we shall see him as he is" (1 Jn 3:2).

Though it is intended to be known in the light of theological faith, dogma, which offers the truths to be believed, depends directly upon the light of prophecy. We certainly cannot speak of one of these lights without speaking of the other. But we can make it our business to describe principally either the life of theological faith or the life of dogma. It is this second aspect with which we shall be specially concerned here.

CHAPTER III

The First Forms of the Prophetic Light

The Different Ways in Which We Are Told
What We Are to Believe

1. Theological faith can exist as a virtuous state, its power dormant and its activity as yet unused, with no need for us to be told what we are to believe. Such is the state of the virtue of infused faith in the soul of a child at the moment of its baptism.

But when faith awakes, when it uses its activity, it must be joined to a truth that is offered for belief. In the natural order it is impossible to think without thinking of something, and in the supernatural order it is equally impossible to believe without believing something.

2. The angels received the prophetic light, showing them what they had to believe of the divine mystery, at the same time as theological faith, and their trial consisted in the choice they had to make between God's darkness and their own brightness.

For men there is no one single way in which the prophetic light manifests what they have to believe.

Under the new law, the divinely assisted Church shows the world what is to be believed, with the fullness it has received from the apostles, who were enlightened by the twofold light of revelation and inspiration. This point must form the central theme of these pages.

Under the Mosaic law the prophets summoned the people ceaselessly to faith in the one God and to hope in his promises.

3. But during the hundreds of thousands of years which preceded the calling of Abraham, during the two thousand years when the gentiles lived on the border of Israel, during the following two thousand years when so many men have lived on the border of the Gospel revelation, what forms has the prophetic light taken?

The Primary Forms of the Prophetic Light

If on the one hand it is God's will for "all men to be saved and to come to the knowledge of the truth" (1 Tim 2:4), and if on the other hand the practice of theological faith is impossible unless we are told what is to be believed, undoubtedly all men, even those who preceded, or had no knowledge of, the revelation of Abraham, or who even today still have no knowledge of the meaning of the Gospel revelation, are yet granted some prophetic light offering to them a message by which they will be saved for all eternity if they accept it in the depth of their hearts. Is it possible in some degree to penetrate this mystery, to try to describe the primary forms in which in the past the message of belief had to be announced, and in which even today it can remain hidden?

The Two First "Credibilia"

The two basic statements needed for the expression of theological faith, or, if you like, the two first *credibilia*, the two "fundamental dogmas", are given us in the great chapter of the Epistle to the Hebrews on faith: "Without faith it is impossible to please him. For whoever would draw near to God must believe that he exists and that he rewards those who seek him" (11:6). These two statements: God exists, God rewards us, represent on the one hand revealed statements, and on the other statements which are basic.

These are statements *whose meaning is revealed.* Reason alone can undoubtedly rise to some knowledge of God and of his providence. But this knowledge, however useful it may be for overcoming obstacles and preparing the way, is not now in question. At the most it can establish the terms of judgments that the prophetic light will enlighten, so as to give them a depth of meaning beyond the scope of reason alone and within the scope only of theological faith. This God who exists, this God who is our providence, is yet the God of Abraham, the God of Isaac, the God of Jacob, not the God of philosophers and learned men. He is the God who begins to reveal, concerning his being and his providence, not merely what can be known through his creatures (Rom 1:20), but things no eye has seen, no ear has heard, no human heart conceived (1 Cor 2:9). He is the God who, in response to this secret message, looks for nothing less than the obedience of faith (Rom 1:5). The twenty-third proposition, condemned together with other errors in moral matters by

Innocent XI, on March 4, 1679, declared that "faith in the broad sense, based upon the witness given by creation, or some other motive of this kind, is sufficient for justification."[1] Faith without which, according to the Epistle to the Hebrews, it is impossible to please God, is of the same kind as that of the patriarchs, Abel, Enoch, Noah, Abraham, Isaac, Jacob, Moses.

The two statements, God is, God is providence, represent statements that are completely basic. They contain in themselves, implicitly, all that will finally be revealed. "All the articles of faith", writes St. Thomas, "are implicitly contained in some primary elements, *prima credibilia*, namely, that God is, and that he is anxious for the salvation of men, according to Hebrews, 11, 6. For in the divine being is contained all that we believe to exist eternally in God, in which our beatitude consists", that is, the mystery of the Trinity, "and in faith in his providence is contained all that God designs in time in order to bring men to this beatitude", and here is the mystery of the redemptive Incarnation.[2] Moreover, St. Thomas explains that those who have not known Christ "have not been saved without faith in a Mediator, for, though they had no explicit faith, yet they had an implicit faith in divine providence, believing that God saves men by ways pleasing to himself; *credentes Deum esse liberatorem hominum secundum modos sibi placitos.*"[3]

---

[1] Denz. 1173.
[2] IIa–IIae, Q. 1, art. 7.
[3] IIa–IIae, Q. 2, art. 7, ad 3.

But have all men been able to know the two primary articles of belief, necessary for all who wish to approach God?

A First Answer of St. Thomas

If God wishes that all men should be saved and if faith is expressed primarily in the two basic "credibilia", must we not conclude that they have been offered in one way or another even to those who have lived apart from the Judeo-Christian revelation, or before it? That is what St. Thomas thinks, and he appeals either to the ministry of angels,[4] or to a direct illumination. Imagining a man brought up in a forest amid wolves, he writes:

> It concerns divine providence to provide every man with what is necessary for salvation, provided he himself puts no obstacle in the way. If, then, the man of whom I speak follows the lead of his natural reason in seeking for good and avoiding evil, we must certainly hold that God will reveal to him by inner inspiration what he must believe (*per internam inspirationem revelaret ea quae sunt ad credendum necessaria*)—or else that he will send a preacher of the faith, as he sent Peter to Cornelius (Acts 10).[5]

The theologians tell us that such illuminations, though they are extraordinary, "should not be considered as miraculous, for they are the natural consequence of the divine will to save mankind".[6]

[4] I Q. 111, art. 1, ad 1; IIa–IIae, Q. 2, art. 7, ad 1.
[5] *De Veritate*, Q. 14, art. 11, ad 1.
[6] Billuart, *De fide*, dissert. 3, art. 2, solv. obj.

A Second, More Profound, Answer

This answer of St. Thomas remains valuable. At the time
he wrote it might have seemed quite sufficient. But St.
Thomas—and this is not the only instance—gave also, as
it were in passing, the principle for a more profound answer
which he found no need to develop, but which is of the
greatest importance today, when human psychology is better known, and when discoveries of prehistory, pushing
back our origins much further, make us regard the spiritual life of our forefathers, vigorous as it may have been,
as cloaked in a kind of unconsciousness.

St. Thomas takes the standpoint of a normal faith, complete and therefore conceptually expressed, whenever he
asks what are indispensable elements that must be believed.
And he replies that always and everywhere it is necessary
to believe explicitly the two primary "credibilia", in which
the mysteries of the Christian faith are implicitly contained, without which the Church would cease to be one
throughout the ages. But previous to this normal state of
faith, is there not the possibility of an imperfect and provisional state in which the two primary "credibilia" would
be believed, truly, actually, formally, so far as their content and substance is concerned, but in a way that is as
yet preconceptual, prenotional, through the will, and to
this extent unconsciously, that is, not with reflective consciousness?[7] The problem is that of the wakening of individual moral consciousness; the answer might be valid also

---

[7] Jacques Maritain, "Le dialectique immanante du premier acte de liberté"
in *Raison et raisons* (Paris, 1947), pp. 131–56.

for the wakening of moral consciousness in the human race.

At a given moment the child, even if we suppose it unbaptized, brought up in a society that is animist, polytheist, et cetera, is compelled to choose for or against rational human good, proper to man. The good to be done, the evil to be avoided, then becomes known to him, though in a confused way, through an idea, a judgment, that is imperative. If he chooses this good, without yet even thinking explicitly either of God or of his final end, what is his state? He is tending at once and directly, even though he is unaware of it, toward that good without which the good proper to man would not exist for a single instant, toward God, the final end of human life. He reaches God actually and formally, but blindly, in virtue of the hidden force of his will, only meeting him and knowing him through following his will to do right. It has been said that,

> the understanding, deprived of its proper resources, can only act below the threshold of consciousness, in a darkness without concept or knowledge that can be expressed. . . . It is a purely practical knowledge of God in the movement of desire for the moral good regarded simply as good. No doubt it involves a metaphysical content, but not grasped as such, not speculatively expressed. It is a knowledge that is purely practical, non-conceptual, unconscious, able to exist in company with theoretical ignorance of God. Thus a man, in virtue of a first free act directed toward the good proper to him, can, without knowing God, tend toward God as the goal of his life, and at the same time know God without being conscious of it, and yet not know him consciously.[8]

8 Ibid.

When this choice is being made, the theologian is aware that the child has not been left to himself by the God who wills that all men should be saved. The sanctifying light has fallen upon him and given him the power to move his will, and the prophetic light the power to change the notion of a good proper to man into a good which will bring supernatural salvation, "by which I shall be saved". If I assent to this notion of a saving good, the real End to which my desire, by means of this notion, is directed is itself supernatural and saving; it is God the Savior. I do not yet know him with a conscious, conceptual knowledge; the knowledge I have of him is for the moment only in the will, and unconscious. Nevertheless it is an actual, formal knowledge, a knowledge full of life. And if I could then conceptualize its content, I should state the two primary "credibilia" as they are formulated in the Epistle to the Hebrews.

The Words of St. Thomas and Their Background

Here is the passage from the *Summa* in which St. Thomas brings out the theological significance of the first human act of an unbaptized child:

> So long as this child has not reached the age of reason, and is not old enough to make use of reason, he remains with original sin alone, and is excused from any actual fault, mortal and, more so, venial. But when he begins to use his reason, his weakness will not suffice any longer to excuse him from all sin, venial and mortal. The first thing which then presents itself to the thought of a man is to

reflect on himself. If he directs himself towards his right end, he will obtain by grace the remission of original sin. But if he does not direct himself towards his right end, so far as he is capable of recognizing it at that age, he will sin mortally, not having done what he was able to do. Then, so long as grace has not purified him entirely, a mortal sin will precede his venial sins.[9]

Now here is the beginning of a study in which this view of St. Thomas is, as it were, rediscovered, and put in its true setting more adequately than ever before:[10]

I consider every first free act, an act whose roots (I may not perhaps recognize it myself: I may become aware of it only by a slight shock, a ripple on the surface of the waters) go right down to the sources of my moral life, where the personality takes itself in hand in order to direct itself to a number of further acts with consequences that may go on indefinitely. Such an act may have been preceded by many others, but it is morally an absolute beginning. . . .

To make this clear let us take the first free act of a child when for the first time it reflects on itself. It reflects. It does not enter upon discursive thought, but it takes itself in hand; it frees or delivers itself from the complete determinism in which it has hitherto lived; it emerges into the moral life, by freely deciding the direction of its life. At the root of such an act there is reflection on itself, which is produced in the understanding, and answers to the question: Why are you living? but without this question being explicitly indicated to the mind. On the contrary it is wrapped up in a choice whose immediate object may be a piece of straw, a mere nothing, yet which involves a

---

[9] IIa–IIae, Q. 89, art. 6. Cf. *De malo*, Q. 7, art. 10, ad 8.
[10] I have tried to put together the conclusions of this study in what should be a treatise on the Church.

spiritual vitality, a decisive importance, a gift of being that a grown-up man will experience in full only on rare and miraculous occasions. *Puerile decus.* Children are told not to play with fire, but they play with God.

Suppose that a child refrains from telling a lie on some occasion in itself quite trifling. He refrains on this occasion, not because he runs the risk of punishment if the lie is found out, or because he is forbidden to tell lies and is afraid of grown-up people, or because he does not wish to incur the danger of giving pain to his mother. He refrains from it because it is wrong. It would not be right to do this. Of course many small actions have already been labelled for him as good or bad by his parents and teachers, and he has been trained by social custom to do the one kind and not to do the other. But this time there is no question of a kind of conditional reflex. When he thinks: it would not be right to do this, it is moral good with all the mystery of its demands, before which he stands as a responsible person and alone, and which is presented to him confusedly in a flash of understanding. And it is the first time that he himself controls his conduct, as a human being, according to the standard of moral good, consciously recognized through an idea, whose power to represent its object is undoubtedly poor and confused, being fitted to a child's understanding, yet whose intuitive intensity, whose validity as knowledge, may be remarkably powerful. Of this event he will not preserve any memory, any more than of the day on which, from the midst of sensible images, the life of reason and of universal ideas awoke in him.

The first deliberate act of will, the first act of moral life in the strict sense, is enveloped in the mystery of grace and of the first sin. In whatever land he was born, whatever tradition he inherits, whether he knows Christ or not, a human child can only rightly begin his moral life in the grace of Jesus Christ. Without this grace, his first free act can only be, as St. Thomas teaches, "a sin that turns him away from his final end".[11]

The Child's First Personal Contact with the Church

Children who have been baptized have been in contact with the Church from the cradle. The Church has taken full hold of them with the sacramental character and the grace of baptism. At the moment when they first come to have a personal encounter with the Church, it remains for them only to take the step which separates habit from act, sleep from awakening. They can do so successfully, since they are set in a privileged position. Nevertheless they can also fail, and wound the Church within them, or, more accurately, wound themselves together with the Church.

In the case of unbaptized children it is indeed in the very process of their first free act that they encounter, not yet the authority, but still the mystery, of the Church. The prophetic light that falls on them to show them the good of salvation, the good by which they can be saved, the sanctifying light that urges them to assent to it, this is already the presence in them of the Church, which is holy and Catholic. If they assent to these lights, they are at once undoubtedly joined, initially, imperfectly, yet in a way that brings salvation, to the great universal Church entrusted here below to the jurisdiction of Peter and of the

[11] Jacques Maritain, "Le dialectique immanante du premier acte de liberté", pp. 131, 146.

sovereign pontiff (they do not know the Church, and neither does she know them by name), of which Christ is
the head (they do not know him, but he knows them by
name). On the other hand, if they turn away from this
light, then it is the Church which they wound in themselves, at the very moment when she tries to save them.

Progress to Notional Knowledge

With this pre-conceptual, pre-notional knowledge, through
the will, of the "good which brings salvation", of the "good
by which I shall be saved", we receive the least degree of
prophetic light necessary in order that theological faith
should be able to come into action and make the understanding really, actually, supernaturally, assent to the mystery of the God who "exists", and who "rewards those
who try to find him".

But this is a provisional, unstable, dangerous, state of
faith, a state of childhood; and knowledge of the mysteries of salvation will require that it should leave the shad-
ows, be perfected, reach an adult state, and find its first
conceptual expression in the two basic "credibilia".

A Condition of Childhood in Man's Membership in the Church

A question arises. Can what I have just said about the
pre-conceptual, pre-notional knowledge through the will
in the child be made to apply to the human race as a

whole? The human race in the course of its psychic and cultural evolution has indeed passed from a condition or phase of magic in which sensations, images, and ideas were obscure, involved "in the dark and changing mental state when the imagination is in control, and when the experience is remarkably vivid but wholly a matter of practical life and, so far as it is an object of reflection, only dreamed about", to the logical condition or phase, in which sensations and ideas are clear, set in "a bright, and settled mental state of the understanding and of its laws of action".[12] Can we suppose that, in the condition of magic passed through by the human race at the time of its mental obscurity, what I have said of the pre-conceptual, prenotional knowledge, through the will, of the primary "credibilia" represented a stage which was normal for it and not, as it may be at the present day, an abnormal and reactionary stage? I think we can suppose this. Without for a moment denying the full knowledge of the primary "credibilia" which must never have utterly deserted the human race, and whose presence we can see in some degree in the theism of pastoral peoples, I think that, when the primitive religions multiplied their myths, there could arise again and again mysterious shafts of light that urged men to consider afresh the meaning of their own lives, showing them the good of salvation by which they might be saved, drawing them to membership in the one City of God, which is the Church. And it seems to me that this condition of salvation represented then, not an abnormal

---

[12] Jacques Maritain, "Signe et Symbole", in *Quatre essais sur l'homme dans sa condition charnelle* (Paris: Alsatia, 1956), p. 84; *Pour une philosophie de l'histoire* (Paris: Seuil, 1957), p. 106.

condition, but simply a condition of childhood as regards membership in the Church.[13]

A Condition of Decay in Membership in the Church

Now that Christ has come and has sent his disciples to preach to all nations, the pre-conceptual, pre-notional knowledge through the will of the primary "credibilia"— apart from the case of the wakening of the unbaptized or uninstructed child to moral consciousness—can represent only an abnormal, regressive condition with regard to salvation and membership in the Church. And yet we know that God, who wills that all men shall be saved and come to the knowledge of the truth, continues, as a result of the redemptive prayer of Jesus, to send these same first rays of light to spiritual regions that have remained closed to the message of the Judeo-Christian revelation. Hence I am convinced that the Church is wider than is supposed, that she possesses everywhere children who do not know her, and whom she does not know. Hence too my deep conviction—not indeed that the gate is not broad or the road wide that leads on to perdition (Mt 7:13), but purely on account of the prayer of Jesus of the greater number of the elect.

[13] "That there is more truth—though concealed—in the religion of early peoples than in the *Religion innerhalb den Grenzen der blossen Vernunft*, is a point I willingly grant to the Chestertonians" (Jacques Maritain, "Signe et symbole", p. 105).

CHAPTER IV

The Old Testament: Homogeneous Development of What Must Be Believed by Means of Fresh Revelations

In the Two Primary "Credibilia" Are Already Contained the Two Supreme Christian Revelations

The two primary "credibilia" already contain the whole substance of the Christian faith: in the revelation that God has made of his being, that which is involved, like a rose in its bud, is the Trinity; in the revelation of his care for the salvation of men that which is involved is the promise of the redemptive Incarnation.

All that is essential in Christian faith is rooted in these two revelations of the Trinity and the Incarnation, which tell us in the darkness of this world "what God has prepared for those who love him" (1 Cor 2:9).

"Those things are essentially concerned with faith," says St. Thomas,

the sight of which we shall enjoy in eternal life, and those things, which bring us to eternal life. Now two things are offered for our sight, the hidden things of God, whose vision makes us blessed, and the mystery of the human nature of Christ, by which we are brought to the glory of

47

the children of God (Rom 5:2). Hence St. John says: "And
this is eternal life, that they know you the only true God,
and Jesus Christ, whom you have sent" (17:3). Therefore
the first distinction in what must be believed will be
between those things that concern God's majesty and those
that concern the mystery of Christ's human nature, which
St. Paul calls the mystery we worship (1 Tim 3:16).[1]

Under these two most general beliefs are grouped all the
articles of the Creed.

In Its Advance from the Primary "Credibilia" to the Christian Revelation, What Must Be Believed by Faith Does Not Increase Substantially but Only by Further Explanation or by Being Made More Precise

We can find a natural analogy to this advance.[2] The notion
of being includes in its universality the notions of one, true,
good, and beautiful, which are not external to it, for outside of being there is nothing. In order that it may be made
more explicit through these notions, the notion of being
does not increase in its substance and content, but simply
insofar as it is more fully explained and made more precise.

So, too, with what is revealed. "So far as the substance
of the articles of faith is concerned," says St. Thomas,

> it is not increased by the passage of time; all that has been
> believed later was contained in the faith of the early fathers,
> though implicitly. But so far as further explanation is
> concerned, the articles of faith have increased in number.

[1] IIa–IIae, Q. 1, art. 8.
[2] Cf. St. Thomas, IIa–IIae, Q. 1, art. 7.

For some things have become known explicitly in later times which were not known explicitly at the beginning. Hence the words of the Lord to Moses (Ex 6:3): "I am the LORD. I appeared to Abraham, to Isaac, and to Jacob, as God Almighty, but by my name the LORD I did not make myself known to them". And the words of David, Psalm 119:99: "I have more understanding than all my teachers." And those of the Apostle (Eph 3:5): "the mystery of Christ, which was not made known to the sons of men in other generations as it has now been revealed to his holy apostles by the Spirit." [3]

Let us not make a mistake here and fall back into the error mentioned at the beginning of these pages, namely, that the statements of faith are not an object of faith. To say that the two primary "credibilia" have not changed substantially in their advance through the centuries does not mean only that their term, the reality which they express—that is, God and his love for men—has not changed, as is obvious; it means that what the two "credibilia" signify has not been transubstantiated by being further explained, that it has developed in a homogeneous, and not an evolutionary, way, that advance has occurred in the well-known phrase which may be already applied here, within a single affirmation, a single meaning, a single truth, *in eodem dogmate, eodem sensu, eademque sententia.*

Doctrine Is Made Explicit Only by Means of Fresh Revelation

The way is a long one that, passing through Abraham, Moses, and the prophets of Israel, reaches from the revelation of the primary "credibilia" to that of the Trinity

[3] Ibid.

and the Incarnation.[4] If the advance occurs in a homogeneous way, within a single viewpoint, a single truth, that which is made explicit within this single viewpoint or truth nevertheless will involve as many surprises as fresh initiatives. Here we see a characteristic of the development of what must be believed, which continued throughout the whole time before the coming of Christ and which ended with the death of the last apostle. In other words the content of the primary elements to be believed can be developed only through the action of fresh prophetic lights of revelation; the advance of doctrine demands fresh revelations.

The revelation of the "God who is" lets the depth of what is meant appear. This God is wisdom, and this wisdom, which is described as his daughter and almost personified, will unexpectedly prepare for the revelation of the Word. He is also Spirit; his spirit covers the original waters to give them life, to give life to the dry bones in Ezekiel's vision, to instruct the prophets, and thus is prepared, always unexpectedly, the revelation of the Holy Spirit.

The revelation of "God who rewards" lets us see in Hosea the incomprehensible love with which he watches over men, and it prepares, again unexpectedly, for the revelation of God who "so loved the world that he gave up his only-begotten Son, that whoever believes in him should not perish but have eternal life" (Jn 3:16). The point upon which the Messianic prophecies converged appeared only when Jesus came to fulfill them. Christianity, it has been said, "did not come, and could not come, from the old

---

[4] For the thought of St. Thomas, see IIa–IIae, Q. 174, art. 6.

Revelation by means of pure rational interpretation. So long as St. Paul interpreted the Old Testament by himself and as a pharisee, he remained a pharisee. To have a true understanding of it, he needed a fresh revelation, that of Jesus Christ." [5]

Throughout the Old Testament, and right up to the death of St. John, the faith goes on, always within a single initial revealed body of teaching, from one fresh statement to another, from surprise to surprise, from revelation to revelation.

The Difference between Advance of Doctrine by Means of Fresh Revelation and Advance by Means of Pure Development

If we are speaking of doctrine to be believed, there is, then, according to St. Thomas, no "substantial" advance, but only further "explanation". But this explanation, this passage from implicit to explicit, differs so far as it either requires fresh revelations, or occurs by simple development.

There are two very different degrees in what is implied by implicit. One is so profound that, while in itself truly objective, yet in relation to human reason it is as though it did not exist, since reason and human powers are unable to explain it or make it clear: divine revelation is needed. In this way the dogma of the Trinity is contained in the dogma of the existence of a supernatural God, or the dogma of the Incarnation is contained in the dogma of God who rewards. These truths, while certainly of themselves implicit, are not implicit in relation to us; they receive the name of

[5] M.-J. Lagrange, *Le judaïsme avant Jésus-Christ* (Paris: Gabalda, 1936), p. 589.

basic dogmas or articles of faith, because they can only be
known by fresh revelations. It is this implicit character which
God has explained more and more clearly throughout the
Old Testament, and this is why, though there was no substantial advance in the Old Testament but only further
explanation, there was advance by means of fresh basic
articles, and consequently advance by fresh revelations. This
explanation ended with Jesus Christ and the Apostles: *haec
explicatio completa est per Christum*.

There is another degree in what is implied by implicit.
Without consisting merely in a verbal explanation, this is
not so profound as to require a revelation. An example is
the dogma of the two understandings and two wills in
Jesus Christ, which results from the dogma of his two perfect natures. Or the dogma of the Immaculate Conception of Mary, which results from the dogma of her being
the mother of God. So, too, with all the truths implicit in
the New Testament after the apostles.[6]

Here we have advance not by fresh revelations, but by
simple development of revelation.

Advance of Revelation and Advance of Dogma

If we make a distinction between articles of faith and truths
of faith, revelations and dogmas, we shall say that up to
the time of Christ and the apostles the advance in what
was to be believed took place by means of fresh revelations, fresh articles of faith, or, if you like, fresh basic dogmas, and that after the apostles the advance in what was to

---

[6] F. Marin-Sola, O.P., *L'évolution homogène du dogme catholique* (Fribourg, 1924),
2:40–41.

be believed took place by means of fresh developments, fresh truths of faith, fresh derived dogmas.

"At the present day in nearly all the manuals articles of faith are each called a dogma of faith. This way of speaking, apart from being wrong, is a great hindrance to the understanding of St. Thomas and our classical theologians and to the formation of a true idea of the immense dogmatic advance after the time of the apostles."[7]

We can return, then, to the two stages in the advance of doctrine presented for belief and can speak on the one hand of advance in revelation, and on the other hand of advance in dogma.

---

[7] F. Marin-Sola, 2:42.

CHAPTER V

The Presentation of Doctrine for Belief in the Apostolic Period and Its History up to the Post-apostolic Period

Here we must at once make a distinction between two stages or forms: the way in which the doctrine for belief was received by the apostles was quite different from the way in which it was received by the Church contemporary with them.

How Was the Doctrine for Belief Proposed to the Apostles?

What was the outward event? Most often the apostles were taught by Christ directly: he gathered them round him to preach the beatitudes on the mountain (Mt 5:1); he explained to them the parables (13:26), announced his passion to them (16:21), told them of his return in glory at the end of time (24:30); for forty days before his Ascension he told them about the Kingdom of God (Acts 1:3). But sometimes, too, the apostles handed on to one another the teaching of their master; only three of them accompanied him at the raising of the young daughter of Jairus (Mk 5:37), at the Transfiguration (Mt 17:1), and at the agony (26:37); Thomas was not with the disciples when Jesus appeared to them in the evening of the Pasch (Jn 20:19); Paul handed on to the Corinthians what he had himself received (1 Cor 15:3). But this outward teaching, direct or indirect, forms only a covering; in itself it could not make apostles.

What was the inward event? Inwardly the apostles at once received a prophetic light of revelation, *apocalypsis*, that showed them in a higher way the meaning of Christ's mystery and by doing this made them apostles: "Paul, a servant of Jesus Christ, called to be an apostle, set apart for the gospel of God" (Rom 1:1). It is a prophetic light coming to them either from Christ still in their midst—at the time of his mortal life or after his Resurrection—or from Christ already returned to his Father to send them his Holy Spirit, as the Pentecost of Vézelay represents him.

At Caesarea Philippi Jesus, answering Peter, said to him, "Blessed are you, Simon Bar-Jona! For flesh and blood has not revealed this to you, but my Father who is in heaven" (Mt 16:17). In the light of such a revelation many acts and words of the Savior were to be made clear, when they looked back on them, in the minds of the apostles. What did Jesus mean when he announced that the Temple of God in the highest sense, that is, his own body, would be destroyed and raised up again in three days? The apostles could not understand (Jn 2:22; 20:9). Neither the entry into Jerusalem on Palm Sunday (Jn 12:16), nor the occasion when he washed their feet (13:7), could at once make them understand. They had to wait until Pentecost: "These things I have spoken to you, while I am still with you. But the Counselor, the Holy Spirit, whom the Father will send in my name, he will teach you all things, and bring to your remembrance all that I have said to you.... I have yet many things to say to you, but you cannot bear them now. When the Spirit of truth comes, he will guide you into all the truth" (Jn 14:25–26; 16:12–13).

The revelation at Damascus was to be the Pentecost of Paul. When he handed on what he had received, it was by grasping it in the brightness of this wonderful light. The gospel he preached to the Galatians was not, he says, inherited or learned from man, but came to him "through a revelation of Jesus Christ" (Gal 1:12), even before he could meet the other apostles (1:17). He reminds the Ephesians "how the mystery was made known to [him] by revelation ... of Christ, which was not made known to the sons of men in other generations as it has now been revealed to his holy apostles and prophets by the Spirit" (3:3–5). It was not as a prophet, for the prophets did not always know the meaning of what they announced, it was as an apostle, working at the foundation of the Church (2:20), that there was bestowed on Paul the privilege "to preach to the Gentiles the unsearchable riches of Christ, and to make all men see what is the plan of the mystery hidden for ages in God who created all things" (3:8–9).

The apostles, who were sent to hand on to the world the wonderful knowledge which they had of the mystery of Christ, were helped by the prophetic light of inspiration, *théopneustie*, to express it in statements communicable either by word of mouth or by writing. But plainly they possessed a greater understanding of the message in their own minds than could exist in the formulation of it they could give to their hearers. There is the same difference between the doctrine for belief as understood by the apostles and as recalled by their disciples, as there is between the master's understanding of what he teaches and the pupil's understanding of what he is taught. It is the supreme dignity of the apostolic knowledge, which the Church intends to safeguard, when it condemns the proposition (the twenty-first of the decree *Lamentabili* of June 3, 1907): "Revelation as constituting the object of Catholic faith is not completed with the apostles."[1]

How Was the Doctrine for Belief Proposed to the Church at the Time of the Apostles?

Under the powerful light of apostolic preaching the disciples were rendered capable of receiving the Gospel message, both oral and written. We may suppose that toward the end of the apostolic period all the essentials of this message had been put down in Scripture, so far as this summarizes the oral teaching in the midst of which it was formed. Without doubt, Scripture is the child of circumstance, but we know that God is the master of events and that nothing of what was written was written except as planned by his will.

The Church at the time of the apostles could read Scripture only in the context of apostolic preaching. To this message, hitherto unknown, whose purpose is at last to provide a final opening for theological faith, it clings through the best of its children, in a way that is intense, forceful, and infallible. Here are to be found all Christian

[1] Denz. 2021.

revelations, all articles of Christian faith: God and the depth of his riches, his unfathomable decrees, the meaning and destiny of the universe. With the preaching of Jesus and the apostles we are at the center of time. Henceforth, and until the moment of the final Parousia, there will be no other fresh revelation to tell us what is to be believed by divine faith. The advance of revelation was finished at the death of the last apostle.

How Was the Doctrine for Belief Proposed in the Post-apostolic Church?

1. What was the aim of theological faith, without which it is impossible to please God, when the apostles had disappeared, when Paul was no longer present to correct the errors of the Thessalonians concerning the end of the world, or of the Corinthians concerning the Supper of the Lord and the resurrection of the dead, or of the Romans concerning justification and the destiny of the Jewish people? Faith itself of course, being a theological virtue, never goes wrong, but the believer, in whom it dwells, can go wrong; he can lose sight of the transcendence of the doctrine for belief, let it become confused, mixed with false elements, and he can finally even lose his faith.

2. But it may be said: "Is not the canon of Scripture final? Is it not self-sufficient? What need have we for an authority to interpret it?" [2] To this St. Vincent of Lérins has a twofold answer. First he says,

[2] St. Vincent of Lérins, *Commonitorium*, 2, 2.

The meaning of Scripture is so profound that all do not understand it equally or completely. The same words are interpreted differently by different people. It may almost be said that there are as many interpretations as receivers. Novatian explains it in one way, Sabellius in another, Donatus again in another, Eunomius, Arius, and Macedonius have their opinion; Photinus, Apollinaris, and Priscillian have theirs; so too Jovinian, Pelagius, and Celestius; finally Nestorius has his.[3]

And here is his second answer:

Do not heretics invoke the witness of Scripture? Undoubtedly they do; they invoke it vehemently. We find them running rapidly from book to book throughout the holy Law, from Moses to the books of Kings, from the Psalms to the apostles, from the Gospels to the prophets! Among their friends, amid strangers, at home and outside, in their sermons and in their books, at meal times and in public places, almost everything they assert they begin by defending with the authority of Scripture.... Thus they undoubtedly imitate the deceptive method of their master.... Is not the devil accustomed to quote Scripture? Read the Gospels: then the devil said to him, If thou art the Son of God, cast thyself down to earth; for it is written, He has given charge to his angels concerning thee." [4]

3. If God wished to preserve publicly throughout the ages without change the original meaning of the revealed deposit, oral as well as written, there was only one way to do this: it was to accompany publicly throughout the ages the revealed deposit with an interpretation which had God's help. This he has done. When Christ sent the Eleven into

[3] Ibid., 2, 3.
[4] Ibid., 25, 1, and 14; 26, 1.

the world he told them: "All authority in heaven and on earth has been given to me. Go therefore and make disciples of all nations; . . . and behold, I am with you always, to the close of the age" (Mt 28:18–20).

4. The divine deposit, which the apostles through the twofold prophetic light of revelation and inspiration had alone been charged to lay down, was entrusted by them to their disciples, through this prophetic light of divine help promised by Christ, with instructions to preserve it living and unchanged throughout the ages: "O Timothy, guard what has been entrusted to you. . . . Guard the truth that has been entrusted to you by the Holy Spirit who dwells within us" (1 Tim 6:20; 2 Tim 1:14).

5. When it passed from the apostles to their disciples, the teaching function of the Church underwent a change in the order of priority. So long as the apostles were living, the authority of the Church was above the statements and formulations of Scripture in which it was expressed; on the other hand for all the post-apostolic period the authority of the Church is not above Scripture but below it: the Church raises Scripture above itself, much as it raises up Christ at the processions of Corpus Christi. Nevertheless it is above the interpretations which men give to Scripture. To the minister, Paul Ferry, Bossuet made this reply: "We do not say that the Church can judge the word of God, but we hold that it can judge the different interpretations which men give to God's holy word." [5] Before this time St. Francis de Sales told Theodore Beza: "It is not Scripture which needs rules and sources of light outside

[5] Edit. Bar-le-Duc, 5:320.

itself, it is our interpretations which need these.... We do not ask whether God understands Scripture better than we do, but whether Calvin understands it better than St. Augustine or St. Cyprian."[6]

6. In Scripture received by the theological faith of the early Church, with the meaning that it had in the light of the oral preaching or tradition of the apostles, and summing up their teaching, lies finally the divine deposit entrusted to post-apostolic authority, which is divinely assisted in order to pass it on from generation to generation.

After the "vertical" transmission or tradition, which passed from Christ to the apostles and to the primitive Church, came the "horizontal" tradition which passed from the primitive Church to ourselves.

---

[6] *Œuvres complètes*, Annecy, 1:206.

CHAPTER VI

The Life of Dogma: Preservation and Explanation of the Revealed Deposit

The Deposit Is Explained by Being Handed On

The handing on of the deposit involves its explanation. For there are two kinds of deposits, lifeless deposits, such as a gold bullion, which is kept just as it is, and living deposits, such as a plant or a child, which are preserved by being allowed to grow. The evangelical deposit is of this kind.

"The doctrine of the faith, which God has revealed," says the First Council of the Vatican, "has not been proposed to men's minds to be perfected like a theory of philosophy. It is a divine deposit entrusted to the spouse of Christ to be kept faithfully and declared infallibly. Hence that meaning of the holy doctrines is to be kept for ever, which our holy mother, the Church, has once declared, and we must never depart from this meaning on the pretext, or in the name of a higher understanding." [1] And the Council here quotes the words of St. Vincent of Lérins: "Therefore let the understanding, the knowledge, the wisdom, of each and all, of every man and of

---

[1] Session 3, chap. 4; Denz. 1800; cf. can. 3, Denz. 1818.

the whole Church, throughout the ages, increase and develop with the greatest vigour, *multum vehementerque*, but only in accordance with their own nature, that is, in the same teaching, the same meaning, the same truth, *in eodem scilicet dogmate, eodem sensu, eademque sententia.*" [2] A little further on the same Council makes it clear that the Holy Spirit has been promised to the successors of Peter, "not indeed by way of revelation, that they may declare a fresh doctrine, but by way of assistance, that they may keep with holiness, and explain with faithfulness, *ut sancte custodirent et fideliter exponerent*, the revelation handed down by the apostles, that is, the deposit of faith".[3]

Thus on the one hand that which was contained in the original deposit explicitly is ever kept in mind by the living authority of the Church, while, on the other hand, that which was contained in the original deposit implicitly, still in a preconceptual, unformulated way, obscure, yet forceful and unavoidable, is explained and put forward in a conceptual and formulated way by the living authority of the Church. Revelations give place to dogmas, articles of faith to truths of faith.

The Preservation of the Deposit

The first care of the Church is to preserve faithfully throughout the ages the deposit which she has received

[2] *Commonitorium*, 23, 3.
[3] Session 4, Denz. 1836.

from the apostles. She has divine assistance for this end. Her authority is enlightened by the prophetic light which helps her; the humblest faithful are raised up by the sanctifying light of theological faith. It is in the fellowship of a community gathered from the beginning under the power of the spirit of Christ, joined together in a single, supreme hope by her worship, her organization, and her will to give witness that she brings to us the Scripture with its whole text, all its meaning, and all its claims. It is not a Scripture uprooted from its true environment, but a Scripture whose fulfillment has begun and is active and alive.

The Church spreads Scripture abroad through her preaching, her professions of faith, and her liturgy. For this purpose it must be translated and set out in different languages. These are not yet developments, but simple reassertions of the revealed truth. The word "person", says St. Thomas, is not found in either the Old or the New Testament in reference to God, but what this word means is found throughout: God is in the highest sense he who is, he who knows, he who loves, and so on. And he adds: "If we had to speak of God only according to the letter of Scripture, we should have to keep strictly to the original languages of the Old and New Testaments." [4] We merely reassert the revealed deposit when we say that God created heaven and earth out of nothing and freely, that the Word was made man, that the Son of Man became incarnate for us and for our salvation, and so on.

[4] I, Q. 29, art. 12, ad 1.

The Sense in Which We Should Return to an Understanding of Our Origins (Ressourcement)

1. These great reassertions, these great redefinitions express the basic doctrines, the articles of our Christian faith. Nothing more sublime, more true, or more holy, can ever be declared here below. In them is contained, as the stream is contained in its source, all that will be finally made manifest of the Christian mystery. They convey of course a meaning that is explicit and capable of being grasped at once; but they are so rich, so concentrated, so full of implicit meaning, wrapped up in them and not yet made clear, that they can never be fully expressed with all their implications and must ever go beyond any expression, as intuition goes beyond conceptualization, and the premise goes beyond the conclusions.

To them we must constantly return; we must immerse ourselves in them in order to rediscover, without being false to them, the substance and the vigor of the revelation of Pentecost. They contain in their wonderful simplicity all the dogmas, all the truths of faith, which will in the end be defined under the pressure of circumstances. Much will need to happen, and much time to pass, if this advance is to take place. But it will never be an advance due to fresh revelations, as it was before Christ and the apostles. The powers of man, enlightened both by the prophetic light of God's assistance, and also by the sanctifying light of faith, will be enough. It will be an advance due to fresh unfolding of the revelation already given. We shall not speak any more of advance in "revelation" or in "articles of faith", but of advance in "dogma" or in "truths of faith".

2. From this point of view, we can understand the constant need of the return to an understanding of origins, spoken of today.

We can also understand very well how illusory it would be to conclude that we can make use of such a return in order to grasp together all the legitimate development of dogma accomplished during twenty centuries under the prophetic light and the light of theological faith whereby God helps us, and to suppose that we can rediscover, by means of purely human disciplines: archaeology, philology, exegesis, history of religions, contemporary philosophies, the meaning of "what no eye has seen, nor ear heard, nor the heart of man conceived, what God has prepared for those who love him" (1 Cor 2:9).

Finally we see how to answer those who, from the Protestant side, blame us for not distinguishing clearly enough between the basic doctrines and the derived doctrines of the Christian faith, the "revelations" and the "dogmas", the "articles of faith" and "the truths of faith". We know how to distinguish between the source and its derivation, but we hold that the doctrine is homogeneous as it passes from one to the other, that the same Love which conveys to us infallibly the revelation through the apostles, preserves it infallibly for us through their disciples.

Development of Doctrine: A Passage from St. Vincent of Lérins

After having insisted in his *Commonitorium* on fidelity to tradition, St. Vincent of Lérins suddenly brings up the question of the advance of the faith:

But perhaps someone will say: Is not then religion capable of any advance in the Church of Christ? Of course there must be advance, and notable advance. Who would be such an enemy to mankind, so hostile to God, as to try to oppose this? But we must stipulate this, that the advance forms a true advance for the faith, and not a change; the characteristic of advance, *profectas*, is that each thing should grow while remaining itself, the characteristic of change, *permutatio*, is that a thing should transform itself into another thing. Therefore let the understanding, the knowledge, the wisdom . . . of the whole Church grow and advance with the advance of the ages, but . . . in the same teaching, the same meaning, the same truth, *in eodem scilicet dogmate, eodem sensu eademque sententia.*[5]

It is not only of an advance in faith in the hearts of the faithful, but it is clearly rather of an advance in its expression of doctrine that St. Vincent is thinking.

Advance in Revealed Doctrine Cannot Be Opposed without Betraying the Doctrine

It is a truth for all men of every period that God, "who desires all men to be saved and to come to the knowledge of the truth" (1 Tim 2:4), makes a revelation directly to some men at a particular moment of time so that, on the one hand, so far as its concrete manner and circumstances are concerned, the divine revelation is always historic and suited to a given situation, while on the other hand, so far as its doctrine frees us and saves us, it is

[5] *Commonitorium*, 23, 1–3.

always "suprahistoric" and independent of any particular "situations".

It follows that a fidelity to the revelation which consists in confining it to its immediate context may be caused by a simple lack of love for essential truth and may become, sometimes perhaps on the pretext of paying it due respect, a pure betrayal of it, the letter killing the spirit. Being outside any particular culture and receiving divine assistance to reach all generations, the divine truth must be able to prove its identity through the ages, and to reply without quibbling when the question is asked, for instance, whether Jesus is only a man, or whether he is the Son of God subsisting in two natures. But to reply to such inquiries is to make explicit the doctrine that has been revealed.

To Make Explicit Is Not to Put Different Statements Side by Side, but to Uncover the Meaning

To make explicit is not to put human comments side by side with the divine deposit, but to uncover its real content, hitherto veiled. We must contrast with a mechanical setting side by side that kind of addition which is vital, as when the tree blossoms; or more precisely, that kind of addition which consists in explanation or making explicit, as when the definition of the circle or the triangle leads to a statement of their properties, without appeal being made to any other information. As to the passages in Deuteronomy (4:2) and Revelation (22:18) forbidding any addition to revelation, the ancients distinguished between an addition of fresh material, always forbidden, and an addition consisting in the implicit becoming explicit, which alone is legitimate. To be accurate, we ought not to speak of addition in this latter case, but simply of explanation. To say that the Spirit proceeds from the Father, writes St. Thomas, is also to say that he proceeds from the Son, since the Father and the Son differ in nothing, save in the fact that the one is Father and the other is Son. But to reject the errors of those who deny this, the procession of the Spirit from the Father and the Son, or from the Father through the Son, has been expressed in the Symbol "not as an addition, but as an explicit explanation of what it contained implicitly; *non quasi aliquid additum, sed explicite interpretatum quod implicite continebatur*".[6]

Being accomplished under the light of infallible assistance promised to the Church, such a passage from implicit to explicit gives birth to dogma. Should we, then, speak of new dogmas? They are new, not by their substance or content, but by the way in which they express and manifest this substance or content. The early Church did not of course know them expressly, but she knew their source, the articles of faith from which they have been derived. Far from disavowing them as they now are, she would rather realize that she had always held and confessed them in their root and principle: as the man who has always refused to decide between two opposed theses, when suddenly faced with the truth in which they are reconciled, may say with full justice that he has always thought it, always believed it.

---

[6] *De potentia*, Q. 10, art. 4, ad 13.

Down the ages, it has been to safeguard the transcendence of the truths of faith, as first formulated in the gospel, against conscious or unconscious rationalizations that dogmas have been defined. We now endeavor to show this by means of a few examples.

CHAPTER VII

Some Examples of Dogmatic Development

The Dogma of the Trinity

From the beginning it is the fundamental dogma of Christianity, that of the Trinity, which has been called in question. We read in the Gospel that we are to give life and baptize "in the name of the Father and of the Son and of the Holy Spirit" (Mt 28:19). We read that "God so loved the world that he gave up his only-begotten Son that whoever believes in him should not perish but have eternal life" (Jn 3:16). This Son is the Word who was at the beginning of time, and who was with God, and who was God (1:1). We read again that the Son will ask the Father and he will send "another Counselor, . . . the Holy Spirit" (14:16, 26).

We certainly wish to accept all this. But, nevertheless, we know without doubt that God is one, and that he cannot present himself to us as contradicting himself, as destroying himself. Without, then, offending the reason he has given us, and which is a chief image of himself in us, how can we hold that there is any real plurality in the divine unity?

It is here that, in order to defend the gospel truth from the accusation of contradiction, we enter upon the path of rationalization. Some, with Sabellius and the Modalists, suggest that the words Father, Son, and Holy Spirit do not refer to God in himself, but only refer to the modes of his action, which is in turn creative, saving, and sanctifying: thus all is clear and comprehensible, but at the same time all is rationalized. It is no longer true that God so loved the world as to give to it his only Son. Others, with Arius, in order to maintain the real distinction between the Father, who is God, and the Son, feel themselves forced to make of the Son a creature, the first of all creatures. Again all is clear and all is rationalized, but it is no longer true that it is the Word-God who was made flesh in order to dwell among us.

What is the Church to do? Is she to withdraw? Is she to let herself dissolve the gospel message in Greek culture? Instead, within Greek culture she asserts her undying faith in Jesus Christ: "only Son of God, eternally begotten of the Father, God from God, Light from Light, true God from true God, begotten, not made, one in Being with the Father. Through him all things were made."[1] The Church confesses the fullness of the Trinitarian mystery: "We worship one God in the Trinity and the Trinity in unity; without confusing the Persons, without dividing the substance; other is indeed the Person of the Father, other that of the Son, other that of the Holy Spirit. But the Father, the Son, and the Holy Spirit have one same divinity, an equal glory, a same eternal majesty."[2] At once there is made explicit the notion valid for all time of subsistent, intratrinitarian relations. To those who maintain that if there is only one God, and if the Father is God, the Son cannot

---

[1] Council of Nicaea; Denz. 54.
[2] Symbol *Quicumque*; Denz. 39.

be God, the Church will point out that it is rash to draw the conclusion that, since the notions of Father and Son are really opposed to one another, therefore they are unable to be identified with one another in the same godhead, and that it is foolish to wish with such presumption to upset the gospel mystery of one God, who has given his only Son. "O learned men," said St. Gregory Nazianzen to the Arians, "the name of Father is not a name for essence; it refers to a relation, the relation of the Father to the Son, and of the Son to the Father. In the Trinity we must say that *other* [*alius*] is the Father, *other* the Son, *other* the Holy Spirit, from fear of confusing the Persons. But we must not say that *another* thing [*aliud*] is the Father, *another* thing the Son, *another* thing the Holy Spirit; for the three are one and the same thing as regards godhead." [3]

Thus to those who claimed that the Church, by preaching the Trinity and the divinity of the Word, substituted for the Gospel message a message which was meaningless, and offered to save it by rationalizing everything, the Church replied once for all that the Trinity and the divinity of the Word are ineffable mysteries, baffling the reason, above reason, but which can never be shown to be unreasonable, contradictory, or meaningless. There is a great gulf between the darkness of faith which is above reason and the darkness of the meaningless which destroys it.

---

[3] PG 36:96; 37:180. As to the axiom: two realities, both identical with a third, are identical with one another, Aristotle had already pointed out that this is no longer true when the two realities, which are identical *re* with the third, differ from one another *ratione*, and are opposed not to the third, but to one another, *oppositione relativa*. See Aristotle, *Physics*, 3, 3, Didot, pp. 275–76; and St. Thomas I, Q. 28, art. 3, ad 1; art. 4, ad 5.

The Christological Dogma

1. On the one hand the Gospel bears witness that the Word, who is God, "became flesh" (Jn 1:14); Jesus himself says: "I and the Father are one" (10:30); "He who has seen me has seen the Father, how can you say, 'Show us the Father'? Do you not believe that I am in the Father and the Father is in me?" (14:9–10). And on the other hand, it is written: "If you loved me, you would have rejoiced, because I go to the Father; for the Father is greater than I" (14:28). There is the last great cry: "My God, my God, why have you forsaken me?" (Mk 15:34).

He is God, and he is forsaken by his God: how can we reconcile these two statements? On the one hand, in order to insist on the divinity, some weaken the humanity; on the other hand, in order to insist on the humanity, some separate it from the divinity, distinguishing a Son of God and a Son of Mary. Each of these two views represents the triumph of easy solutions and of rationalism; as a result of each the gospel is torn to pieces.

What is the Church to do? If she does not intend to withdraw—and she wished this no more at Chalcedon in 451 than at Nicaea in 325—only one way is open: to make fully explicit and for ever the transcendent revelation of the Word made flesh:

> We all agree in teaching one and the same Son, our Lord Jesus Christ—the same perfect in divinity and perfect in humanity, true God and true man, the same, made of a rational soul and a body—consubstantial with the Father as to divinity, consubstantial with us as to humanity, fashioned as we are, only sinless—begotten of the Father before

all ages as to divinity, but in the last days for our sakes and for our salvation born of the Virgin Mary, Mother of God, as to humanity—one and the same Christ, Son, Lord, only-begotten, whom we recognize to be in two natures, without confusion, without change [against the Monophysites], without division or separation [against the Nestorians], the difference of natures not being removed by their union, but rather the properties of each of the two natures remaining whole, and meeting in a single person or hypostasis—not separated or divided into two Persons, but one and the same Son, the God-Word, only-begotten, the Lord Jesus Christ, as formerly the prophets taught concerning him, and then Jesus Christ himself taught, and as the symbol of the fathers has handed down to us.[4]

Why should all these precise statements be made? Only to close in advance the way for those tempted to rationalize the unfathomable mystery of the one Savior Jesus, refusing to admit either the fullness of his divinity or the fullness of his humanity.

2. What happened, in the year 55, "in the church of God at Corinth"? St. Paul speaks of a table that is an altar, of a bread that is the body of the Lord, of a cup that is the blood of the Lord; of a union of the faithful with this body and this blood by eating and drinking, just as the Jews partake of the sacrifices of the Mosaic law, and the gentiles of the sacrifices to idols. But neither the sacrifices of the gentiles nor the sacrifices of Israel are any longer allowed, on pain of provoking the jealousy of the Lord. Here is the passage:

[4] Denz. 148.

The cup of blessing which we bless, is it not a participation in the blood of Christ? The bread which we break, is
it not a participation in the body of Christ? Because there
is one bread, we who are many are one body, for we all
partake of the one bread. Consider the people of Israel;
are not those who eat the sacrifices partners in the altar?
What do I imply then? That food offered to idols is anything, or that an idol is anything? No, I imply that what
pagans sacrifice they offer to demons and not to God. I
do not want you to be partners with demons. You cannot
drink the cup of the Lord and the cup of demons. You
cannot partake of the table of the Lord and the table of
demons. Shall we provoke the Lord to jealousy? Are we
stronger than he? (1 Cor 10:16–22)

If the "bread" and the "cup" of Christ are not offered to
God in sacrifice, what remains of this argument of St. Paul?
A little further on he similarly says that, on the night when
he was being betrayed, the Lord Jesus asked his disciples
to enter into his sacrifice with him through love, and
through eating and drinking, receiving within themselves
the bread which is his body, and the cup which is his
blood, until the day when he will come again (11:23–27).
If St. Paul is not here a victim of myth, if he tells us what
he "received from the Lord", if his account is divinely
inspired, surely we find again unchanged the fullness of
this extraordinary revelation in the teaching of the Council of Trent. According to this Council the Savior wished
to draw the Church within the drama of Redemption by
asking her to renew at Mass the unbloody sacrifice of the
Last Supper, "by which the bloody sacrifice once to be
offered on the Cross should be *represented*, and its memory
should *remain* to the end of the ages, and its saving virtue

should be *applied* for the remission of the sins we commit every day.... The fruits of the bloody offering being obtained in abundance by the unbloody offering; so far is the latter from derogating from the former in any way." [5] Hence the Mass appears as the real entry of each generation, one after another, into the sacrificial drama of the Passion, in which each has its place prepared in advance.

3. "Now as they were eating, Jesus took bread, and blessed, and broke it, and gave it to the disciples and said, 'Take, eat; this is my body.' And he took a chalice, and when he had given thanks he gave it to them, saying, 'Drink of it, all of you; for this is my blood of the covenant, which is poured out for many for the forgiveness of sins. I tell you I shall not drink again of this fruit of the vine until that day when I drink it new with you in my Father's Kingdom" (Mt 26:26–29). The Church adds nothing to the meaning of these words. She accepts them fully. If it is true that God so loved the world that he gave to it the bodily presence of his only Son, the Church thinks that he could love the world enough, if this is not of itself impossible, to leave it the bodily presence of this same only Son. And, since on the day of the Ascension Christ left us to rise into heaven, where he appears in the form proper and natural to him, it is clear that he could only be present here bodily in a mysterious manner, and appear in a form, strange and borrowed. The primary intuition of the Church, from which the whole eucharistic dogma comes, is that of a bodily presence of Christ, who wills to be among us until the Parousia, hidden under the appearance of bread and wine, in

[5] Session 22, cap. 1 and 2; Denz. 938, 940.

order to allow us to share, like his disciples at the Last Supper, in his bloody sacrifice on the Cross. We find it defined by the Council of Trent:

> And because Christ, our Redeemer, has said that what he offered under the appearance of bread was truly his body, therefore there has always been this belief in the Church, and the holy Council declares it again, that by the consecration of the bread and wine there takes place a change of the whole substance of the bread into the substance of his body, and of the whole substance of the wine into the substance of his blood. This change has properly and rightly been called by the holy Catholic Church *transubstantiation.*[6]

The canon that corresponds makes it clear that there is reference to a change that is unique:

> If anyone should say that, in the most holy Sacrament of the Eucharist, there remains the substance of the bread and wine together with the body and blood of our Lord Jesus Christ, and should deny this wonderful and unique change of the whole substance of the bread into the body, and of the whole substance of the wine into the blood, only the appearance of bread and wine remaining, a change fitly called by the Catholic Church transubstantiation, let him be anathema.[7]

To deny this doctrine it would be necessary to deny the truth of one of the three following propositions: first, "this is my body"; second, this is no longer bread; third, the visible appearance of bread has not changed. The first of these three propositions is directly revealed; the second is

[6] Session 23, cap. 4; Denz. 877.
[7] Denz. 884.

revealed in the first, for, if the bread remains, the proposition "*this* is my body" is false, and the true proposition would be "*here* is my body"; the third proposition is immediately evident. *The mystery of the continuation* of the bodily presence of Christ among us is closely connected with *the mystery of the coming* among us of the Word made flesh. If, in order to get rid of such puzzling revelations, we suppose that the Gospel only wished in certain places to speak in images, it is Christianity as a whole which suffers.

The Marian Dogma[8]

1. Mary, as we see her in the Gospel, is mother of Jesus who is God, not only in a bodily way, but freely, consciously, with full knowledge of what she did, still more with her soul than with her body. She is equal, so far as is possible for a mere creature, to the holiness of her mission. *She is the worthy mother of the Savior God.* Since the heresies forced the Church to proclaim the divinity of Jesus, Mary is proclaimed Theotokos. This is the concept upon which the attention of the Church centers with infallibility, and from which are deduced by a valid process of unfolding all the privileges of the Virgin.

2. It is a central truth of Scripture that no one at all can be holy or be sacred except by the redemption of Christ. If the Virgin is redeemed, is it not from some sin? The Oriental Church Fathers—Origen, Basil, Cyril of Alexandria—think first of some doubt which could have

[8] See my *Esquisse du développement du dogme marial* (Paris: Alsatia, 1954).

entered her soul at the foot of the Cross; it is a way that leads nowhere. The West, where the doctrine of original sin was carefully studied, found itself faced with a dilemma: either the Virgin is redeemed, and this can only be from original sin, or, in order to exempt her from original sin, we must decide to withdraw her from the redemption of Christ. How, then, could the Church use her infallibility? Only through the notion, which came to be suggested, of a *redemption*, not which *purified* her from the original stain, but which *preserved* her from it: "By a special grace and privilege of almighty God, and in consideration of the merits of Jesus Christ, Savior of the human race, the blessed Virgin Mary has been, at the first moment of her conception, preserved and exempt from any stain of original sin." [9]

3. After this the definition of the Assumption of the Virgin was imminent. For it is revealed, according to St. Paul, that for the members of Christ stained with original sin, the law of conresurrection, or at least of conglorification ("We shall not all sleep, but we shall all be changed": 1 Cor 15:51) in Christ is held back until the end of the world—that is to say, until the moment when original sin, as being sin of the whole of human nature, is fully overcome: (a) by the cessation of generation, which propagates it, and (b) by the resurrection of all those whose death it will have caused: "the last enemy to be destroyed is death" (1 Cor 15:26). But by this it is also revealed at the same time that, for a member of Christ not stained by original sin, the law of conresurrection (or of conglorification) in

---

[9] Pius IX, Bull *Ineffabilis Deus*, December 8, 1854; Denz. 1641.

Christ will not find any hindrance, and will at once be applied, as in the case of Christ: "We pronounce, declare, and define", says Pius XII, "this dogma to be divinely revealed, namely, that the Immaculate Mother of God, Mary, ever a Virgin, after having finished the course of her earthly life, has been assumed, body and soul, into heavenly glory." [10]

4. What is contained *explicitly* and revealed *immediately* in Scripture is, on the one hand, the necessity of redemption for all men and, on the other hand, the utterly exceptional holiness of the Virgin Mother of Jesus, who is God. What is contained *implicitly*, but really, and revealed *mediately* in Scripture, and now *explicitly* formulated, is—with regard to the Virgin Mother of Jesus who is God—her redemption, which kept her free from original sin, and her glorious Assumption, which follows as a corollary.

What the early Church grasped firmly was that Jesus is the Word made flesh. What she grasped with the same firmness of faith was that the Virgin Mary is, both in body and soul, the worthy Mother of Jesus, the God who is Savior of the world. She grasped nothing else expressly either of the Immaculate Conception or, we may add, of the Assumption; she had no idea of this. Her treasure of Marian certainty was wholly compressed in an invincible and *absolute power of denial* with regard to anything that could offend in any way the supreme dignity of the Theotokos, the Panhagia. When in the course of time there was suggestion of a doubt to which the Virgin might have given way at the foot of the Cross, or of an indiscretion of

---

[10] Pius XII, Bull *Munificentissimus Deus*, November 1, 1950.

which she might have been guilty at Cana, or later of an original stain, all that the Church could say, with the vigor of divine faith, was *No!* And, as the simple effect of this "No!", without anything else, all the assertions of Marian dogma were established.

CHAPTER VIII

Dogmatic Formulas and Common Sense

Dogmatic Assertions in Terms of Common Sense

These concern first of all the reassertions of *facts* recorded in Scripture: the Virgin Mary is Mother of Jesus who is God. Jesus suffered under Pontius Pilate. He underwent physical death, he rose again the third day of his own power, he rose from the tomb, and so on.

They concern also the translation in direct terms of what was said in Scripture in terms of *images*: the arm of God means the power of God; the descent into hell means the salvation of redemption applied to the just of earlier ages; the Ascension and sitting at the right hand of God mean the sovereignty of Christ in glory,[1] and so on.

Technical Formulation of Dogma

But the teaching authority of the Church has been led to give to the faith a technical formulation, though without ever subjecting it to any system. Thus it does not seek to

[1] With regard to the descent of Christ into hell and his Ascension into heaven, see *Nova et Vetera*, 1963, no. 3, pp. 191–215.

enthrone any philosophic doctrine, but on the other hand it seeks to bar the way to any attempt at rationalization, however subtle, to uphold in its full integrity, and to its full extent, we may say with all its scandal, the unimaginable meaning of the Gospel words: "the Word was God", "the Word was made flesh", "Take, this is my body", and so on. Anxious to dispel deviations and to attack them in their final strongholds, it does not hesitate to give a technical formulation to the true belief, which alone can exclude ambiguity. It continues spontaneously to act like the Fathers of the first centuries, who, in order to safeguard the transcendence of the revealed deposit against attempts at rationalization and syncretism and to define the great trinitarian and christological dogmas, had to give technical precision to the notions of paternity and filiation, of generation and procession, of subsistent relation and of consubstantiality, of person and of nature. When they began to examine these *critically in the light of faith*, and freed them from all that was not their direct concern, they made use of conceptual elaboration which they judged proper for making explicit the original revealed doctrine. When necessary they themselves invented terms to serve the faith; they made the faith manifest, they did not in any way dominate it.

The Reality Defined by Dogma Can Be Grasped either on the Level of Spontaneous Knowledge or of Elaborated Knowledge

The dogmas, in which are expressed the great Christian mysteries, while remaining identical in their essential meaning, in their universal validity, can be grasped on two levels of our intellectual knowledge, on the level of spontaneous knowledge and common sense, and on the level of elaborated and reflective knowledge.

At both of these moments it is the same reality which is grasped, the same unfathomable revelation to which the mind of the believer assents according to the degree of intensity of his own faith. At the first moment, however vigorous it may be, the knowledge is still *general and shadowy*; it outlines the zone of the mystery in a confused fashion, like the sun hidden in a mist. It is instinctively, when searching for the answers in the depths of his heart, that the believer settles the difficulties which face him—for example, a mother questioned by her child about the Christian truths she is teaching him. At the second moment, the knowledge gains in *precision and clearness*; it does not of course get rid of the mystery, and it is aware that it would be sacrilege to pretend to rationalize. On the contrary, it is in the hope of paying it higher honor, of separating it from what is foreign to it, of being able to answer, even technically, the questions it raises, and finally of opening a clearer path to faith, that it strives to outline it.

Hence it is true that dogma begins by being expressed in formulas of *common sense*. It makes use of the meaning they directly convey. This is enough to clarify the knowledge of the faithful and to open to them widely the gates of love. But it is not true that it cannot, and should not, reach a higher degree of precision. To whatever extent error is refined, dogma pursues it to its lair. It is then formulated in language which is *elaborated and technical*. But it does not cease to dwell within the spontaneous understanding, and in this sense does not cease to remain accessible to it in a certain degree. There is no esoteric doctrine in Christianity.

There Is No Esoteric Doctrine in Christianity

1. That by being "elevated" the deep meaning of mysteries can be rendered accessible to common sense is the subject of a chapter,[2] in which, starting from the notion of human personality, P. Garrigou-Lagrange, by drawing out the full conclusions, introduces his reader to the very heart of the mystery of the Incarnation. Let me quote the following page:

> The *individuality* that distinguishes us from beings of the same kind is derived from the body, from the matter that occupies a particular amount of space distinct from that occupied by another man. By our individuality we are essentially dependent on a particular background, climate, heredity, Greeks, Latins, Saxons. Christ was a Jew. *The personality*, on the other hand, is derived from the soul. To develop one's individuality is to live a selfish life of the passions, to make oneself the center of all, and finally to end by becoming the slave of the countless passing goods which provide us with a momentary, unhappy, joy. On the other hand, the personality grows in so far as the soul, rising above the sensible world, attaches itself more firmly through the understanding and the will to that which makes up the life of the spirit. Philosophers

[2] *Le sens commun, la philosophie de l'être et les formules dogmatiques* (Paris: Beauchesne, 1909), pp. 163–69.

have glimpsed, while the saints especially have understood, that the full development of our poor personality consists in losing it in some sense in that of God.... Thus they have acquired the most powerful personality that can be conceived, they have in a sense acquired that which God possesses naturally: independence of all creation, not only independence of the physical world, but independence of the world of understanding. As Pascal has said: "the saints have their empire, their glory, their victory, their splendor, and have no need of bodily or spiritual greatness; these have no connection with them, adding nothing and taking nothing away. The saints are seen by God and the angels, and not by bodies or curious spirits: God suffices for them...." Christ himself, Man-God, is seen as the term toward which holiness vainly strives to tend. Ultimately it is no longer only in the order of *operation* that the human ego gives place to a divine person; it is in the very order of *being*, root of operation. Hence it is literally true to say that the personality of Jesus is the personality even of the Word, and that he subsists with the subsistence of the Word,[3] with whom he makes up one and the same being. Such is the ultimate reason of that stupendous personality of which history never has, and never will, show a likeness. Such is the ultimate reason for the majesty of that ego which belongs only to Christ: *Ego sum via veritas et vita. Venite ad me omnes et ego reficiam vos* ...

In the same place it is shown, by other examples, that, even when expressed in philosophical language, the dogmatic formulas remain within the range of common sense.[4]

---

[3] *Subsistentia* = personality.

[4] A way in which the mind may be elevated concerning the mystery of the Trinity is proposed by A. Gardeil, *Le donné révélé et la théologie*, pp. 140–43.

2. Bossuet turns our eyes toward the birth of the Word:[5]

Why should God not have a son? Why should that blessed
nature lack that perfect fruitfulness which it gives to creatures? Is the name of Father so shameful and unworthy of
the first Being that it cannot belong to it by natural fit-
ness? Shall not I that make others to bring forth children,
myself bring forth? (Is 66:9). And, if it is noble to have, to
become, children by adoption, is it not still more noble
and great to beget children by nature?

I know well that an immortal nature has no need, as
ours has, being mortal and feeble, to renew itself and per-
petuate itself, so as to put in our own place children whom
we leave in the world when we depart from it. But in
itself, apart from this necessary replacement, is it not noble
to produce another self, through richness and abundance,
as a result of a union which is inexhaustible—in a word,
through fruitfulness, and the richness of a nature which is
happy and perfect? . . .

Though a man and a son of man can be imperfect, a
God and a son of God cannot be. If, then, we free the
Son of God from this imperfection, what else remains but
that which was said by our fathers at the Council of Nicaea,
and from the beginning of Christianity, that he is "God
of God, Light of Light, true God of true God", perfect
son of a perfect father, of a father who does not depend
upon the years for his fruitfulness, but is always father,
never without a son. . . .

Again, God the Father has not any need to be united
to anything other than himself, in order to be a father
and to become fruitful; he does not produce this other
self outside himself; for nothing of that which is outside
God is God, and thus God conceives in himself; he carries in himself his fruit which is eternal with himself.

[5] *Elévations sur les mystères*, second week.

Though he is only father, and though the name of mother does not befit him, yet he has a womb, as though he were a mother, in which he bears his son: "From the womb of the morning, he says, I begot you" (Ps 108:3). And the son is called "the only-begotten Son, who is in the bosom of the Father" (Jn 1:18). . . . He who is borne in a measureless womb is from the very first as great and as measureless as the womb in which he is conceived, and he never comes forth from the womb which bears him.

God will never have any but this son, for he is perfect, and he cannot have another; a single childbirth of this perfect kind exhausts all the fruitfulness, and draws all the love. That is why the Son of God calls himself the only-begotten Son, *Unigenitus*.

This singleness of spontaneous understanding and Gospel preaching, *this kinship of the faith of the simple and of the highest Christian revelation*, has always been accepted by the fathers and the doctors of the Church.

Dogma Is Not Made Subject to Any Culture

Even when formulated in scientific language, dogmatic definitions, as I have said, do not subject dogma to a system, a philosophy, or a culture. They may borrow notions like that of nature, relation, substance, or person, from metaphysical systems, but they do so while neglecting the context in which they belong, while criticizing them in accordance with the demands of faith, carrying them into a light more excellent than that of all the philosophies.

The objection will certainly be made: If the terms of these formulas go beyond the limits of common sense, what guarantee is there of their unchangeable validity? The Church herself is the guarantee, the organ of Christ, which, in her infallibility, has judged of the analogical validity of concepts expressed by these terms. Far from *subjecting itself* to these concepts, Revelation *makes use* of them, it *uses them as in every order the higher makes use* of the lower, in the philosophical sense, that is, it orders them to its own end. Supernature *uses* nature. Before making use of these concepts and these terms, Christ, through the Church, has judged them, and approved them in a wholly divine light, which is not measured by time but by unchanging eternity. These concepts, plainly inadequate, could always be made more precise, but never given up. Thus defined dogma cannot *let itself be assimilated* by human thought in perpetual evolution; such assimilation would only be corruption. On the contrary it is dogma which wishes *to assimilate* this human thought which only changes ceaselessly because every day it dies. It wishes to assimilate it in order to communicate to it here below something of the unchanging life of God. The truest believer is he whose understanding is most thoroughly passive in regard to God.[6]

To the objection of subjection of dogma to ancient philosophy, an answer has recently been given by simple reference to facts:

In Christian thought the fathers and doctors have as their one care to be faithful to the thought of the Church, and not to deviate from this thought. They do not seek to invent an original system. Quite the opposite, they reject this. They seek to think with tradition. They constantly refer to their predecessors. They refer especially to holy Scripture, which is their rule and their standard. We may say that, running through them all there is a collective

---

[6] P. Garrigou-Lagrange, op. cit., p. 189.

thought which is being worked out, the thought of a Body. ... Orthodox Christian thought, in the first centuries, *chose* in Greek philosophy the elements which seemed to it serviceable, and it rejected metaphysical theories which seemed incompatible with its own principles, its own demands. That is to say, in fact *Christian thought rejected the more original and more common theories of ancient metaphysics.*[7] Hence we are very far from a pure and simple invasion of Christianity by Greek philosophy, as a number of historians have supposed that they found.[8]

[7] For example in asserting the non-eternity of the world, the freedom of creation *ex nihilo*, the eschatological destiny of the universe, the resurrection of the body, etc. See on this the fine book of Pierre de Labriolle, *La réaction païenne, Étude sur la polémique antichrétienne du 1er au vi^e siècle* (Paris: 1934).

[8] Claude Tresmontant, *Les idées maîtresses de la métaphysique chrétienne* (Paris: Seuil, 1962), p. 15.

CHAPTER IX

The Truth Value of Revealed Statements

Absolute Truth of the Doctrines of Faith

The statements of faith concerning God and his works tell us that which is, they apply to reality, however mysterious may be its depths; they are true with an absolute truth. Whether they are revealed immediately as "articles of faith", or revealed mediately as "dogmas" in which these articles are made explicit, and whatever may be the context of events which have been able to determine their appearance, they are messages addressed to us by him who *is the Truth*. It is upon them that he has required us to hazard our life and our death; it is upon their speculative and metaphysical value that is based their practical and moral value.

We betray them, if we claim that they do not refer directly to divine reality; that they express it only under the forms of vital reaction which correspond to them in ourselves; that, for instance, the assertion, "God is personal", means simply: "Behave yourself in your relations with God as in your relations with a human person"; in short that "the dogmas of faith should be accepted only in the practical sense, as standards of conduct, not as standards of belief." [1] For faith, "God is good" has not a merely *negative* meaning, removing from him all evil, nor a merely causal or *functional* meaning, describing him as cause of the goodness of things: God is good in himself *previously to all reference to the world.* It is not at all because he has created the world that he is good, says St. Thomas, it is because he is good that he has created the world: [2] "No one is good but God alone" (Lk 18:19). It is by no means because he has given life to men who are intelligent and free that God is a person, it is because he is sovereignly subsistent, intelligent, free, and thus sovereignly personal, that he has given life to men whom he has made to his own image and likeness (Gen 1:26). It is because he is Father, in a manner eternal and extraordinary, that from him "every family in heaven and on earth is named" (Eph 3:15).

We cannot repeat too often in these days of agnosticism, in one sense we know God far better than we know the men with whom we live most intimately. The man who shakes hands with me will perhaps decide at the same time to betray me; his gesture may be false, I can doubt his word, his virtue, and his goodness. On the other hand I know with absolutely certain knowledge, even by my reason alone, that God cannot lie, that he is infinitely good, infinitely just, infinitely holy. Of all beings it is he in one sense that I know best, when I recite and meditate on the Lord's Prayer, as it is by him that I am best known. [3]

[1] This is the twenty-sixth proposition condemned by the decree *Lamentabili*, July 3, 1907; Denz. 2026.
[2] I, Q. 13, art. 2.
[3] P. Garrigou-Lagrange, op. cit., p. 151.

Love lives with the absolute. We do not tell a woman that it is of no importance to her to know whether her husband is faithful to her, or a man that it is of no importance to him to know whether the child given him is really his own, that it is enough to act "as if" it was. We do not tell a Christian to act "as if" God truly became incarnate for love of us, "as if" Jesus gave himself bodily to us when we receive Holy Communion. And does God himself wish to be loved *functionally*, on account of the gifts that he gives us, or does he wish to be loved *for himself*?

Variations in Terminology without Variations of Meaning and Vice Versa

It is the *meaning* of the revealed statements that is important and that, as I have said, falls within faith. The *words* in which this meaning is expressed may vary—that is obviously so when they are translated into different languages—owing to the fact of the transcendence of spiritual thought in relation to its material means of expression. Hence it may happen that the same expression, rejected in the sense it first possessed, should afterwards be adopted by the faith with a substantially different meaning. When the word *consubstantial*, for example, was rejected at the Council of Antioch in 264, it was in the sense given it by Paul of Samosata, who meant through it to preach Modalism, and, while asserting their consubstantiality, to deny any real distinction between the Persons of the Father and the Son. On the other hand at the Council of Nicaea in 325, when the Eusebians entrenched themselves behind the biblical expressions which described the Son as "the image of the invisible God" (Col 1:15), "the glory of God and bears the very stamp of his nature" (Heb 1:3), in order to assert his "likeness" to the Father, but to deny his divinity (Jn 1:1; 20:28; Rom 9:5; Tit 2:13) and his equality with the Father (Jn 10:30), the non-biblical word *consubstantial* becomes the only word which can disown their sophistical exegesis, and declare both the identity of nature of Father and Son, and at the same time their personal distinction, since, as St. Basil remarks, "a reality is never consubstantial with itself but always with something else." The word "consubstantiality", at first rejected as covering over an error, is later adopted as an expression of the faith. There is variation of terms, but absolute fidelity to a single thought which is made precise.

The opposite situation is far more common. It is the Christian terms which are then maintained, but only to be reinterpreted. The words creation, Incarnation, redemption, Real Presence, transubstantiation, justification, mystical body, and so on take on new meanings. We have only to recall what has become of the Apostles' Creed from the Hegelian or simply the Modernist point of view. All the words are there, like an empty husk carried about by the winds of history and ideologies at their pleasure.

Advance in the Expression of an Unchanged Doctrine of Faith

We may speak, though in this very exact sense, of a "historic relativity" of the statements of faith.

1. According to St. Augustine, "the earlier plenary councils are often corrected by the later plenary councils when experience causes what was closed to be opened and what was hidden to be known, *aperitur quod clausum erat et cognoscitur quod laiebat*".[4] The word "to correct", *emendare*, here, remarks Pierre Batiffol, means a development:

> When a bishop was rebuked by a regional council, it was because there had been in the letters or discourses of this bishop something which deviated from the truth, deviated in the sense of the English "went astray", *si quid a veritate deviatum est*. There is no question of a plenary council going astray, departing from the truth, so as to be put right by a subsequent plenary council: there is only question of its not seeing what a subsequent council would see, because the truth, contained or latent in the received faith, was often made clear thanks to the controversies which broke out, which followed, which reached their necessary end.[5]

Augustine elsewhere suggests the example of the word *homoousion*, consubstantial, which is not in Scripture, "which the faith of our fathers invented, which the Council of Nicaea confirmed, which catholicity has defended".[6] Here he anticipates the thought of Vincent of Lérins.

2. I have already quoted the well-known passage of the latter, which contrasts with transformation, *permutatio*, of the faith, its advance, *profectus*, in the same dogma, the same meaning, the same truth.[7] Here are two other passages where the same concern is expressed:

---

[4] *De baptismo*, bk. 2, chap. 3, 4.
[5] *Le catholicisme de saint Augustin* (Paris: Gabalda, 1920), p. 39.
[6] *Refutation of Two Pelagian Letters, to Pope Boniface I in Four Books*, I, 3.
[7] *Commonitorium*, 23, 1–3.

You have received gold; it is gold that you must give back. I do not want you to substitute one thing for another. I do not want you shamefully to give me lead or fraudulently to give me copper instead of gold. I do not want that which resembles gold, but real gold. O Timothy, priest, expositor, doctor, if divine favor has granted you the talent, experience, and learning, be the Beseleel of the spiritual tabernacle (Ex 31:2). Cut the precious stones of divine dogma, set them faithfully, adorn them wisely, add to them brilliance, grace, and beauty. Through your explanations, let that which was formerly believed more obscurely, be understood more clearly, *intelligatur industrius quod antea obscurius credebatur.* Thanks to you may future generations congratulate themselves on having understood what past generations venerated without understanding. But teach the same things that you have learned. Say the things in a fresh way, yet without saying fresh things, *ut cum dicas nove, non dicas nova.*[8]

Here is another passage: "It is right that those ancient dogmas of the heavenly philosophy[9] should be cut, smoothed, polished as time goes on; it is wicked to transform them, *commutentur,* to mangle or mutilate them. Let them receive more clearness, light, precision, *evidentiam, lucem, distinctionem*; but let them be sure to retain their fullness, their wholeness, their own meaning, *plenitudinem, integritatem, proprietatem.*"[10]

3. The teaching of the Fathers is that of St. Thomas: "The truth of faith is sufficiently explained in the teaching of Christ

[8] Ibid., 22, 5–7.

[9] "The expression 'heavenly philosophy' only seems to be established toward the end of the fourth century; it is common in St. John Chrysostom, who contrasts the spiritual state of true Christians, directed toward heaven, with that of men who are still attracted by the world." Michel Meslin, *Saint Vincent de Lérins,* Ed. Soleil levant (Namur, 1959), p. 105.

[10] *Commonitorium,* 23, 13.

and the apostles. But, since wicked men pervert the apostolic teaching and Scripture (see 2 Pet 3:16), an explanation of the faith has become necessary in the course of time." [11] "The decision of a general council does not take away from a subsequent council the power to produce a new edition of the symbol [creed], not indeed containing another faith, but the same faith better expressed, *magis expositam.*" [12]

4. I have quoted the passage in the First Vatican Council, which teaches that "the meaning of the holy dogmas that must always be retained is that which our holy mother the Church has once recognized in them, and this it is never right to turn aside from, on the pretext of, or in the name of, a higher understanding, *altioris intelligentiae specie et nomine.*" [13] We may recall to mind the solemn definition corresponding, in canon 3: "If anyone says that it is ever possible, as a result of progress in knowledge, that a sense should be given to the dogmas set down by the Church other than that which the Church has understood and understands, let him be anathema." [14]

Could the thought of the Church about the absolute truth of the statements of faith be more clearly expressed?

Are the Following Ideas True or Not?

May I be allowed to set down three examples of recent dogmatic interpretation without mentioning the names of

[11] IIa–IIae, Q. 1, art. 10, ad 1.
[12] Ibid., ad 2.
[13] Session 3, ch. 4, Denz. 1800.
[14] Denz. 1818.

their authors, and leaving the reader the task of deciding whether they are faithful or not to the doctrine of the faith.

1. The first concerns the Eucharistic presence. I quoted above the solemn declarations and definitions of the Council of Trent. Here is the account which is offered of this mystery:

> Against the background of Scholasticism, which has lost the notion of a thing as a sign, and which regards the reality of the thing as the substance, which makes up the foundation beneath the accidents, the thing could only change really if the substance changed, and then the transformation necessarily becomes transubstantiation. In a universe looked at against the background of Augustinianism ... we may conceive that a thing, being by God's will the sign of a thing other than that which it is by nature, may itself become other, without its appearance being changed. The appearance remains, but the purpose, the function, the character of the thing as sign having changed, the thing itself has changed really, since its function, which is to signify, is the most profound element in its ontological reality.... Before the Consecration the bread and wine have, like everything else in nature, a religious meaning and being. But when, in virtue of the offering of them made according to a rite determined by Christ, they become the efficacious symbol of the sacrifice of Christ, and hence of his spiritual presence, their religious being is changed. Through the creative will of God, they have been made entirely new. Thus they have undergone a transformation, and of the most profound kind, since they have been changed on that level of being which constitutes them in their true reality. This is what we can mean by transubstantiation.

Consequently the "scholastics" and, with them, the Fathers of Trent have lost sight of the notion of thing as sign (*res et signum*), and have simply confused a change of *purpose* (whether profane or religious) in the bread, with a change of the bread's *being*. A *functional* change has become for them a *substantial* change. It is to the former, to the merely functional change, not to the latter, that we should now apply the word, which the Catholic Church declared most suitable, *transubstantiation*.

2. The second example concerns the primacy of the sovereign pontiff. Here is the declaration of the First Council of the Vatican: "If anyone says that the Roman pontiff has only a duty of inspection or of direction, and *not a full and supreme power of jurisdiction over the whole Church, not only in things which belong to faith and morals*, but also in those which belong to the discipline and government of the Church, or *that he only has a more important part, but not the whole fullness of this supreme power . . . let him be anathema*."[15] But on April 6, 1415, when three pretenders disputed for the tiara, and when one of them, the pseudo-John XXIII, was in flight, the Council of Constance solemnly declared the superiority of the ecumenical council over the Pope.

What is the truth? We know the answer of the theologians: a doubtful Pope, no Pope, *papa dubius, papa nullus*. A universal council gathered to elect a true Pope has no authority except for this one task; it is only perfect so far as the circumstances allow, *secundum praesentem Ecclesiae statum*.[16] The decisions it may be able to make eventually within the scope of its primary purpose will only have ecumenical validity in virtue of ultimate

---

[15] Session 4; Denz. 1831.

[16] Cajetan, *De comparatione auctoritatis papae et concilii*, ed. Pollet (Rome: 1936), no. 229.

confirmation by the Pope it elects. Hence the definition of the fifth session of Constance plainly exceeded the powers of the council, and remained invalid. The fathers of the First Vatican Council, who were aware of this, had no doubt on the matter.

Here, however, the suggestion is made that, since Martin V, elected at Constance, only decided to dissolve the council with its approbation, "the relations between Pope and council could not be more clearly defined in terms of submission of the papal executive to the legislative sovereignty of the council." Consequently, "the two definitions are thus equally true, not only that of Vatican I asserting the superiority of the Pope (which no one doubts), but also that of Constance defining the superiority of the council (which no contemporary theologian hitherto maintained). The antinomy is only apparent, the two kinds of superiority not being the same, but each in its own way an indispensable *service* rendered to the Church of Jesus Christ." *Legislative* sovereignty of the council, *executive* sovereignty of the Pope: what else can we say except that in the express terms of the Vatican I definition, the "full and sovereign power" of the Roman pontiff over the whole Church, far from being limited to executive power, even, indeed primarily, concerns the highest matters, "that which touches on faith and morals".

3. The third example concerns the notion of creation. Canon 5 of the First Vatican Council declares: "If anyone does not confess that the world and everything it contains, spiritual and material, have been produced out of nothing by God in the totality of their substance, *secundum totam suam substantiam a Deo ex nihilo* . . . let him be

anathema" (Denz. 1805). And here is the idea of creation as it has been put forward at the present day:

> In the beginning, then, there were at the two poles of being, God and the Many. And yet God was quite alone, since the Many, sovereignly separated, did not exist. From all eternity God saw beneath his feet, the scattered shadow of his Unity; and this shadow, while being an absolute aptitude to give something, was by no means another God, because it itself was not, nor had ever had being, nor had ever been capable of having being—since its essence was to be infinitely divided in itself, that is to say, to be stretched over Nothing. Infinitely vast and infinitely rarefied, the Many, made nothing by its essence, slept at the furthest remove from Being, which is one and centered about itself.... It is then that the overflowing Unity of Life entered into conflict, by Creation, with the non-existing Many which opposed it as a contrast and a challenge. *To create, if we follow what appears clear to us*, is to condense, to concentrate, to organize, to *unify*.... I do not hide from myself that this conception of a kind of *positive Nothing*, subject of Creation, has to meet grave objections. However stretched over nothing we may suppose it, the thing, being naturally separated and required for the action of creative union, implies that the Creator has found, outside himself, a point of support, or at least of reaction. It thus suggests that Creation has not been entirely gratuitous, but represents an almost absolute work of self-interest. That is true. But is it really possible to avoid these difficulties (or rather these paradoxes) without becoming involved in purely *verbal* explanation? ... In the world as object of "Creation" classical metaphysics has accustomed us to see a kind of extrinsic production, resulting, through overflowing goodwill, from the supreme *causality* of God. Inevitably—and quite rightly if we are to be able both to act fully and to love fully—I am led now (in conformity

with the spirit of St. Paul) to see in it a mysterious work of completion and fulfillment for the Absolute Being himself. *There is no longer Being participating in externality and divergence, but Being participating in fullness and convergence.* Thus there is no longer creative causality, but creative Union!

I post just one question: Is it "classical metaphysics" only which is here being arraigned—or is it the conciliar definition of the free and gratuitous production of everything out of nothing, in the totality of their substance?

CHAPTER X

The Question of Language

The Words of John XXIII

On October 11, 1962, in his opening speech at the twenty-first Ecumenical Council Pope John XXIII intended to give an authoritative answer to the question, *how doctrine may be advanced in our days*:

> The twenty-first Ecumenical Council wishes to hand on in its fullness, without lessening it or distorting it (*non imminutam, non detortam*). Catholic doctrine which, in spite of difficulties and opposition, has become the common inheritance of men. This inheritance certainly does not find favor with all, but it is offered to all men of good will as a rich treasure which they may possess.
>
> Nevertheless, we have not only to preserve this rich treasure, as though we were only concerned with faithfulness to the past (*uni antiquitati*); we must further devote ourselves joyfully and without fear to the work that the present age requires, following the path along which the Church has gone for twenty centuries.
>
> Our first aim is not further to decide certain principal points of the Church's doctrine, and thus to repeat more fully what the Fathers and theologians, ancient and modern, have handed down; we rightly think that these things are not unknown to you, and that they are engraved in your minds.

If only questions of this kind had to be considered there would be no need to gather an ecumenical council. What is needed today is the assent of all, with renewed love, in peace and tranquillity, to the whole Christian doctrine in its fullness, *nulla parte inde detracta*, handed down with that precision of terms and concepts, *tradita accurata illa ratione verba concipiendi et in formam redigendi*, which has been the glory especially of the Council of Trent and of the First Vatican Council. Answering to the lively desire of all those who are sincerely attached to all that is Christian, Catholic, and apostolic, this doctrine must be more fully and more deeply known, souls must be more thoroughly immersed in it, transformed by it. This doctrine, certain and unchangeable, *certa et immutabilis*, to which we owe fidelity and submission, must be examined and presented so as to suit the needs of the present time, *ea ratione quam tempora postulant nostra*. For we must distinguish between the deposit itself of the faith, namely, the truths contained in our venerable doctrine, and the way in which these are set forth, though always with the same meaning and the same thought, *alius modus quo enuntiantur, eodem tamen sensu eademque sententia*. We should attach great importance to the way in which it is set forth, and should work patiently, if necessary, to elaborate this. We should follow the way of presenting these truths which agrees most perfectly with the teaching authority, whose character is above all pastoral, *eae inducendae erunt rationes res exponendi, quae cum magisterio, cujus indoles praesertim pastoralis est, magis congruant.*[1]

John XXIII went on to speak of the *way in which error should be checked*: "The Church has never ceased to oppose errors. She has condemned them often and severely. But today the Spouse of Christ, rather than have recourse to

[1] *Act. Apost. Sedis*, 1962, p. 791.

the weapons of severity, prefers to apply the remedy of
mercy. She thinks that instead of condemnation, she answers
better to the needs of our age if she makes better use of
the riches of her doctrine." [2]

His Meaning

The great purpose of John XXIII, the great mission that
the Holy Spirit urged him to inaugurate, here again, is
clear. It was not for a transformation of doctrine that he
hoped and to which he invited us; it was a transformation of climate. For the climate of disruption, which alone
has allowed the multiplication of differences among Christians, he tried to substitute a climate of reconciliation. So
too for an age-long climate of Catholic presentation of
doctrine, *based primarily, though certainly not only, on its unity,*
purity, coherence, growth, and inward holiness, he was trying
to substitute a climate, new or perhaps older, of presentation, Catholic also, of the pure doctrine defined in the
ecumenical councils—including those of Trent and of the
First Vatican Council—*based primarily on its diffusion* in a
world which is suddenly aware of entering, with the
appearance of striking technical methods, an unknown
period of its history. For at the very beginning of the
preaching of the good news there was a time, when
the aim, though not the only aim—we may remember
the constant warnings of St. Paul and of St. John against
falsifiers of the message, or the rebukes of the Savior to

[2] Ibid., p. 792.

the scribes and pharisees—when the chief aim was to spread it in the world then accessible. There followed a time when the chief aim was to maintain its inward coherence and growth in a culture that had become Christian. Now the time has come—with a pope freed from his earlier temporal responsibilities as head of the Vatican States and as guardian of medieval Christianity—for undertaking a fresh effort at missionary expansion. We see what we are to understand by "new way", "fitted to the needs of our time", "suited to the pastoral care of the teaching authority", of presenting "in its fullness", the "certain and unchangeable doctrine", "defined and expressed with such precision by the ecumenical councils". More than anyone else the missionaries know the difficulty there is in translating into different languages without change the lofty and pure doctrine of Scripture and the catechisms. Woe to those among us who, when opening their mouths to teach the gospel, are never troubled by the thought that they may perhaps be about to betray it! How are we to find the language that will make it penetrate, with its transcendence and its purity, into the "hearts of the masses", which are exposed to all the suggestions of the spirit of the world, and of the "Prince of this world"?

As to the *way in which error may be checked*, the terrible condemnation of Jesus, of the apostles, of the first councils, have continued to be effective, and the *anathema sit* of the apostle (Gal 1:8; 1 Cor 16:22) is found as late as in the canons of Trent and of the First Vatican Council, but this applies to the doctrines, not to persons. For, not possessing prophetic light for the discernment of souls, we know well enough that the final judgment of the drama of a human existence must be left to God. But could this free the Church from her perpetual concern to point out to her children, to the very humble or the very learned, the doctrines by which they may be led astray, or lead their brethren astray? Is it not her cherished duty, her duty as Spouse, to watch over the purity of the truth, to be anxious about anything which can tarnish it? Is not charity concerned primarily with truth, with *the Truth*?

Is Our Language Suitable to Express Revealed Doctrine?

1. Christian doctrine, as we find it at different moments of its existence, in Scripture and in the first councils, among the Fathers of the East and of the West, and among the scholastics, in the Council of Trent and the First Vatican Council, means to tell us "that which is"; it presents itself as an understanding of being, not of the phenomenon or of the *praxis*; it is—and the too significant attacks of some people against what they contemptuously call outdated scholasticism deceive no one—it is an *onto-sophia*.

Our languages are composite: in one respect, and this is an important respect, insofar as they conceal spontaneous views and intuitions concerning being, they are ready to welcome Christian wisdom; in another respect, so far as they reflect the ideology, the propaganda, the changing passions of an age, they are suited for evading Christian wisdom and are very capable of misinterpreting and betraying it.

2. "It is not enough", as has been pointed out in this connection,

to consider language as such in its nature or even in its basic structure; we must also pay attention to the way in which it is employed at a given moment of history. Then certain words, certain expressions, for example, become preponderant. A lived culture is always a phenomenon of choice. It assures a privileged place to perspectives, problems, solutions, authors, a vocabulary, phrases and formulas. The language as used shows the reflection of these choices. And the slogan is perhaps only the residue which caricatures (and today this is deliberately encouraged) a process inherent in every living culture. The messenger who carries to men a wisdom of being could not, in spite of the timelessness of his message, be unaware of these phenomena. Man is a being who is taught. Thus he accepts thought through language. But this is a political reality; it is essential to the *conversatio* that is the city.[3]

This "political" and flowing aspect of language makes it more suitable to express the ideologies of a given moment than the messages of an "unchangeable" wisdom, which invites the soul to silence, and we may guess that the preachers of this wisdom will have always, like the prophets of Israel, the apostles, and the Savior, to retrace in this matter the course of their time.

3. It has been pointed out, for example, that the kind of behavior which characterizes in general the state of understanding in our age of positivism and technology "tends of itself, if we are not careful, to have an unconscious repercussion on the way in which we receive the faith. Preceding any formulation of an atheist philosophy,

---

[3] Marie-Martin Cottier, O.P., "Libres propos sur le blondélisme", in *Nova et Vetera*, 1962, p. 272. See the penetrating remarks on language of Henry Bars, *La littérature et sa conscience* (Paris: Grasset, 1963), p. 203.

sometimes even in philosophies that boast of leaving room
for religion, even of protecting it, there is a kind of behavior of the understanding that is in itself atheist because,
instead of being zealous for being, it eliminates and emp-
ties out being." [4] We do not try to see; our understanding
does not see. We do not go beyond signs, formulas, the
statement of conclusions. We have secured information
about reality, and it will serve us; that is all that we should
do. It is not a question of entering by means of this upon
a view of reality itself. What happens when our faith lets
itself be contaminated by this background, when it takes
the path which is followed by the understanding as it acts
in the modern world?

> Then it becomes *fixed* in *signs*; it does not go forward, or
> does so as little as possible, to the *reality which the sign
> signifies*. Thus it damages those very precious conceptual
> signs, the dogmatic formulas, by which the living God
> speaks of himself in our language, and whose sacred vir-
> tue and dignity depend precisely on the fact that they are
> vehicles of the divine reality. There have always been Chris-
> tians for whom the knowledge that Christ has redeemed
> the sins of the world is a piece of information of the same
> abstract kind as the knowledge that the temperature this
> morning was twelve degrees centigrade. The statement is
> enough for them, just as the reading of the thermometer
> is enough. They quite mean to use this information to
> get to heaven—but they have never come face to face
> with the reality of the mystery of the redemption, of the
> reality of the sorrows of the Savior, they have never expe-
> rienced the shock of the knowledge of faith, the scales
> have never fallen from their eyes. What I mean is that the

[4] Jacques Maritain, *Le philosophe dans la cité* (Paris: Alsatia, 1960), p. 180.

way in which the modern understanding behaves runs the risk of regarding as normal that way of proceeding in the faith which indeed tends of itself to empty out the faith.

Must We Speak the Language of Our Own Age?

Yes, if we do so in order to awake our age to the message of eternity; no, if we do so in order to dissolve this message in the flow of time or evolution and to deaden in man the sense of the absolute.

Yes, if we do so in order to attempt by means of the language of our age—by every language of every age—to make contact in every man with those deep levels where the statements of the revealed message can cause to be appreciated the absolute character of their truth, their demands, and their promise of deliverance.

No, if we do so in order to insert the divine truths in the web of ideologies in which the spirit of an age lives;[5] or in order to make of Christianity—forgetting its transcendence—the normal completion of an evolutionary process in the universe.

---

[5] "Philosophy is identical with the spirit of the age in which it appears; it is not above it, it is only the awareness of what is substantial in its time, or again the thought which knows what there is at the time.... An individual can no more get away from the substance of his time than he can get out of his skin. Thus, from the substantial point of view, philosophy cannot get beyond its time" (Hegel, *History of Philosophy*). There, stated in its full force, is the definition of historicism.

CHAPTER XI

Defacement of Dogma

The Problem

At the beginning of this little book I made a clear distinction between the sanctifying light of theological faith and the prophetic light of revelation, showing how they were related to one another and necessarily complementary. We set ourselves to grasp the elementary forms of the prophetic light which is expressed in the two primary "credibilia", to notice their development first by new revelations, new articles of faith, until the time of Christ and the apostles, then by new forms in which they were made explicit, new dogmas, in the post-apostolic period. Through the infallible light of divine assistance the truth fully revealed by Christ and the apostles will thus continue to be made more explicit to the end of the world.

But the period of struggle between light and darkness, between Christ and Belial (2 Cor 6:15), will end only with the Parousia. Opposite to the revealed doctrine are arrayed the forces of error and destruction. Their only object is to oppose the spread of Christian preaching; they still strive to disrupt it in large portions of the human race and even in the hearts of many of the baptized. The question that arises is thus whether the sanctifying light of faith can resist the mutilation of Christian doctrine and can continue, under conditions no doubt abnormal and often dangerous, really to survive, if not in its full activity, at least in substance. Without hesitation we must answer, Yes.

The Chief Collective Mutilations of Dogma

Starting with those that are dogmatically less extensive, and afterward coming to those that are more and more grave, we may first consider the group of those that have broken away.

It is of first importance to distinguish between heresy and its consequences. *Heresy* is the personal sin of the man who rebels against the faith by deliberately rejecting any one of the revealed truths: a personal sin can never be inherited. It is the *consequence* of a heresy, the *legacy* of a heresy, that is inherited and that we must call a breaking away. Persons who are born in these conditions will become heretics only if they deliberately make their own the original rupture. "He who defends his opinion," says St. Augustine, "however false and perverse, without stubborn ill will, especially when this opinion is not the outcome of pride and presumption, but when it has been inherited from parents led astray and captivated by error, if he conscientiously seeks the truth and is ready to submit to it when he knows it, should by no means be counted as a heretic." [1] In *Orthodoxy* the impact of Christian principles remains considerable and almost complete, and the principle of error, though

---

[1] *Epist.* 43, 1; quoted by St. Thomas, IIa–IIae, Q. 11, art. 2, ad 3.

it represents an incalculable evil, seems comparatively secondary; but in *Protestantism* the principle of error has been able to do great damage to Christian doctrine.

If we turn to the question of *religious bodies who do not acknowledge Christ*, then members of these bodies are still our brethren; they are not brethren "separated" from us within Christianity, but brethren who profess themselves non-Christians, who have never joined us, at least visibly, on the path which we try to follow with Christ.

Some of these bodies acknowledge the monotheism of Abraham. In particular there is Israel, which has not recognized its Messiah, which still preserves the inspired Scriptures, but for which, alas, these Scriptures are covered with a veil (2 Cor 3:13–16). Then there is in a lesser degree—for the inspired Scriptures are replaced by the Qur'an—the monotheism Islam received from that Israel which had already turned aside from its mission. There can be no doubt that acceptance of monotheism in both these forms—even though they may wish to boast of it against the Christian mysteries of the Trinity and the Incarnation—produces in these bodies a religious climate of high quality.

The religious groups *that do not acknowledge the faith of Abraham*, and among which truth and error are mingled, may form *patrimonies or legacies* unfaithful on the surface to the graces of light which God has always sent to all men. But it would be unjust to attribute to all their members the *sin* of infidelity, to see in them all "infidels" or "pagans". Let us speak, with the gospels, of the "nations" or the "gentiles". As Scripture talked of the "Greeks", let us talk of the Hindus, Buddhists, Confucianists, and so on.

The Position of the Individual Catholic
Who Gives up His Belief

The distinction between the inner light of theological faith and the prophetic light which sets forth from without the doctrine for belief, helps us to understand the very delicate problem of the Catholic who gives up his belief.

1. In most cases his inward force has become weak. He had received at baptism the light of theological faith. But little by little he had allowed the suggestions and spirit of the world to enter in. He had not yet committed any precise, deliberate act of infidelity. The faith with its doctrines lived in him. But one day this faith, weakened and diminished, found itself faced with a passion, a revolt. It wavered, and fell. Wrong was done. For, if we call to mind the First Vatican Council, it is "the same most loving Lord who both stirs up with his grace and assists those who go astray so that they may be able to come to the knowledge of the truth (1 Tim 2:4), and who also confirms by his grace those whom he has brought out of darkness into his admirable light (1 Peter 2:9), that they may persevere in this light. He never abandons anyone, if he is not himself abandoned, *non deserens nisi deseratur.*" [2]

2. But when the desire for, and love of, truth remain sound, is it possible that through a mistake, and without any sin against the virtue of faith, a Catholic should join, for example, a heterodox religious body?

---

[2] Session 3, chap. 3; Denz. 1794. These last words are taken from the Council of Trent, session 6, chap. 11; Denz. 804, which quotes St. Augustine, *De natura et gratia*, chap. 26, 29: "God does not abandon those once justified by his grace, unless he has first been abandoned by them, *nisi ab eis prius deseratur.*"

Here in outline is the answer given to this question by P. Gardeil.[3] Some theologians, he says, assure us that without sin a man may not indeed lose divine faith, but may see its objective aspects so changed that the statements of Catholic dogma fail to have their full effect. A similar process appears as a phenomenon of regressive evolution. The First Vatican Council, which pronounced on the matter, simply declared that no one ever has a *just cause* for changing or revoking the faith he has promised to the teaching authority of the Church. This is how the passage continues: "The condition of those who have accepted Catholic truth through the heavenly gift of faith is quite different from that of those who, led by human opinions, follow a false religion. For those who have received the faith by the teaching of the Church can never have any *just cause* for changing it, or for entertaining any doubt."[4] One sees that the Council did not intend to settle the question of knowing whether, yes or no, without an objectively legitimate reason, a Christian can perceive (more or less) before his very eyes, the weakening of certain doctrines of the faith.

The theologians referred to point out that if, according to St. Thomas, the *universal* principles of the natural law (good must be done and evil avoided; we must act in accordance with reason, etc.) can never as such disappear from a man's conscience, the *secondary* principles of the natural law (for example: the obligation to pay debts, the prohibition of violence, of polygamy, etc.) can be wiped away

---

[3] *La crédibilité et l'apologétique* (Paris: Gabalda, 1912), p. 297.
[4] Session 3, chap. 3; Denz. 1794.

from men's hearts. Following the teaching of St. Thomas, they say, then, provided there is no inward refusal to believe, faith can continue, if its *indispensable main object* is present, that is, the object sought primarily by the activity of faith: God at least confusedly known by a supernatural light in the absolute character of our final end and in the claims of truth. But as to the statements that make this *object precise*, and that come to us by external teaching—statements about the Trinity, the Incarnation, and so on—though generally speaking their disappearance from the field of knowledge of the faith is the result of a sin, it may happen occasionally that they are obscured by involuntary and invincible errors, positive faith tending toward its proper end.

3. When faced, then, with the distressing case of a Catholic who gives up his belief, two situations are possible. Often there is culpable ignorance, and then we shall have to try to reawaken in this paralyzed conscience the desire for sovereign truths. Sometimes, however, there may be complete good faith, through ignorance of the signs given by God, for the truth of the Church. What should we do with regard to those souls shown by their conduct to be absolutely sincere? Here are the final words of advice which P. Gardeil gives concerning them:

> If God is with them, if they preserve the spark of divine faith present in them, if they obey the law which they know, even though they feel it is their duty to persecute what they take to be the Church, and to upset the (positive) faith of others, in spite of all this and in spite of the strange consequences, they may perhaps believe more firmly than they persecute. In the depths of their consciences we *may suppose* that there may dwell that basic tendency toward

God, supernaturally known, which is enough, absolutely speaking, for justification, and contains the substance of the faith. And then, if we employ on their behalf the only argument which remains, namely, prayer, we shall try to console ourselves by repeating the words of Paul to Philemon: "Perhaps, after all, the very purpose of thy losing him for a time was that thou mightest have him always by thee." [5]

---

[5] Gardeil, *La credibilité et l'apologetique*, p. 312.

CHAPTER XII

Dogma and Contemplation

Dogma and Mystery

The dogmas—the Trinitarian dogma, the dogma of the utterly free and gratuitous creation of the universe, the dogmas of the Incarnation, of the redemptive sacrifice, of transubstantiation, the sacramental dogmas, the Marian dogma—are the great declarations which the Church has made known against rationalization of the wonderful revelations of Holy Scripture. Far from weakening the mystery, they mark its outlines in order that the spirit may enter further into its darkness and lose itself in its depths.

The Church is divinely assisted by the prophetic light of infallibility in order to present them to us. But it is not on its created authority that we believe—the presentation which the Church offers *conditions* our assent to their truth, it does not provide the *basis* for the assent; it is on the uncreated and direct authority of God, revealing himself to us and revealing to us his work, that we believe. Faith, theological faith, is the inward, personal light by which God comes to the understanding and will of each man, so as, if no obstacle is met with, to raise them to himself. "He who believes in the Son of God has the testimony in himself, *habet testimonium Dei in* se" (1 Jn 5:10); "Who is

it that overcomes the world but he who believes that Jesus
is the Son of God" (5:5).

The Knowledge of Simple Faith

At the first moment when it is received in the soul, the
light of Christianity bestows both the prophetic gifts of
divine revelation and also the power to recognize them,
that is, the sanctifying light of theological faith that causes
us to assent to their mysterious depths and that is thus
seen to be the root of the whole work of justification.[1]
The believer is encompassed by ideas, revealed statements,
in which is expressed his Creed, what he believes about
God and God's work, creation, redemption, salvation, the
last ends. His faith makes use of these statements in an
intuitive, not a discursive, way. It is concerned to make
the whole human person assent to the truth of what they
contain.

Mystical Knowledge

Let us pass on to the second moment. Let us suppose that
the divine light in the believer attains its supreme intensity. Let us suppose that theological faith, fostered by love,
and not content to adapt the soul to the truth of revealed
statements, begins to show that *there is, in the truth of these
revealed statements, still more truth than they can express.* "The

[1] Council of Trent, Session 6, chap. 8; Denz. 801.

light of faith", says St. Thomas, "makes us see the mysteries which are believed";[2] it encounters them, it touches them in some sense in the darkness; it is on the path which divine faith opens out by means of revealed notions that God's love draws the understanding of faith to go beyond these notions. Then it rises upon the wings of love and of the gifts of the Holy Ghost toward those things eye has not seen nor ear heard (1 Cor 2:9); it plunges into a silent contemplation in which all concepts are hushed; it is swallowed up in the mystery of "the depth of the riches and wisdom and knowledge of God" (Rom 11:33). Here, in this supreme act, is the realm of mystical knowledge.

But—and this is the point which must be emphasized at the end of these few pages—conceptual knowledge of revealed truths is not in any way *laid aside*, or in any way got rid of, it is merely for the moment covered over, *transcended*. All the dogmas thus subsist in the faith of the contemplative, but like the stars in the midday sunlight. In fact they are never so necessarily, so effectively present. The passing light which throws them into the shade strengthens them to a wonderful degree. When it withdraws, they reappear like stars in the evening sky, but invested with, and illuminated by, a little of its brightness.

When St. John of the Cross was engulfed in the "midday" of God, which is "midnight" for faith, how was it possible for him to think distinctly and successively of each of the mysteries of the childhood or of the Passion of the Savior? It was a silent contemplation which he was sent to teach the world. But as soon as the dazzling light of unity

[2] IIa–IIae, Q. 1, art. 4, ad 3.

allowed him some respite, he found again distinctly each of these Christian mysteries and was, as it were, inebriated with them. At Baeza he carried in his arms the Child from the cradle, at Avila he sketched out his vision of the Crucified, he was on fire with love as he touched the Blessed Sacrament.[3] A mystical contemplation that, at the moment when it began and ceased, was not ready to allow each of the Gospel mysteries to appear, contained in it like petals in the rose, would not be Christian contemplation.[4]

[3] Bruno de Jésus-Marie, *Saint Jean de la Croix* (Paris: Desclée De Brouwer, 1961), pp. 163, 259, 309; English trans. *St John of the Cross* (London, 1936), pp. 220ff.

[4] Cf. my *Introduction à la Théologie*, pp. 312–13.

SELECT BIBLIOGRAPHY

Batiffol, Pierre. *Primitive Catholicism.* Translated by H. L. Brianceau. London: Longmans, 1911.

Bettensen, H. *Documents of the Christian Church.* London and New York: Oxford University Press, 1943.

Bindley, T. H. *The Œcumenical Documents of the Faith.* 4th ed. London: S.P.C.K., 1950.

Bovis, André de. *What is the Church?* New York: Hawthorn Books, 1964.

Butler, Dom B. C. *The Church and Infallibility.* London and New York: Sheed and Ward, 1954.

Chenu, M. D. *Is Theology a Science?* New York: Hawthorn Books, 1959.

Dvornik, Francis. *The General Councils of the Church.* Washington, D.C.: Dumbarton Oaks, 1966.

Hughes, Philip. *A History of the Church*, 3 vols. London and New York: Sheed and Ward, 1934.

———. *A Popular History of the Catholic Church.* New York: Macmillan, 1962.

Joly, Eugène. *What Is Faith?* New York: Hawthorn Books, 1958.

Journet, Charles. *The Church of the Word Incarnate.* London and New York: Sheed and Ward, 1955.

———. *Wisdom of Faith.* Westminster, Md.: Newman Press, 1952.

Kelly, J. N. D. *Early Christian Creeds.* London and New York: Longmans, 1950.

———. *Early Christian Doctrines.* London: Black, 1958.

Maritain, Jacques. *The Degrees of Knowledge*. New York: Scribners, 1958.

Mercier, Cardinal Desiré. *Modernism*. Translated by M. Lindsay. London: Burns and Oates, 1910.

Newman, Cardinal J. H. *An Essay on the Development of Christian Doctrine*. London: Longmans, 1845.

Rondet, Henri, S.J.: *Do Dogmas Change?* New York: Hawthorn Books, 1961.

Sheed, F. J. *Theology and Sanity*. San Francisco: Ignatius Press, 1978.

Thomas Aquinas, St. *Summa Theologica*. Translated by the English Dominican Fathers. 5 vols. Notre Dame, Ind.: Ave Maria Press, 1948.